我们在浙大留学

主　编　陈　丽

副主编　袁雯静

翻　译　李淑敏　刘晓杰

ZHEJIANG UNIVERSITY PRESS
浙江大学出版社

图书在版编目（CIP）数据

我们在浙大留学 ： 汉英对照 / 陈丽主编 ；李淑敏，
刘晓杰译. -- 杭州 ：浙江大学出版社，2019.7
　　ISBN 978-7-308-19305-4

　　Ⅰ．①我… Ⅱ．①陈… ②李… ③刘… Ⅲ．①留学教
育－概况－中国－汉、英 Ⅳ．①G648.9

中国版本图书馆CIP数据核字(2019)第137325号

我们在浙大留学

主编　陈　丽　**副主编**　袁雯静
翻译　李淑敏　刘晓杰

责任编辑　樊晓燕
责任校对　杨利军　沈倩
封面设计　林智广告
出版发行　浙江大学出版社
　　　　　　（杭州市天目山路148号　　邮政编码　310007）
　　　　　　（网址：http://www.zjupress.com）
排　　版　杭州林智广告有限公司
印　　刷　杭州高腾印务有限公司
开　　本　710mm×1000mm　1/16
印　　张　13.25
字　　数　248千
版 印 次　2019年7月第1版　2019年7月第1次印刷
书　　号　ISBN 978-7-308-19305-4
定　　价　49.00元

曾经，为了追寻中华民族复兴的梦想，我国一批又一批仁人志士出国求学；如今，越来越多的外国学者和青年学生来华交流学习，中国已成为世界第三、亚洲最大的留学目的地国。据教育部统计，2017年有近50万名外国留学生来中国高等院校学习，来华留学生规模增速连续两年保持在10%以上。其中，有近6万名学生享受了中国政府奖学金的资助。

为了主动服务"一带一路"倡议，强化海洋国际合作与交流，2013年浙江大学海洋学院（以下简称浙大海院）联合自然资源部第二海洋研究所[①]（以下简称海洋二所）招收了首批中国政府海洋奖学金留学生，加上浙江大学、海洋二所、导师的筹资助学，通过5年多的努力，已招收了70多名涉海类专业留学研究生。包括本人在内的海洋二所多名学者被聘为浙江大学博士生导师，参与了留学生指导工作，同时通过对留学生的培养加深了与国外原有的合作研究，拓展了新的合作，使海洋二所的国际合作平台更宽、对推动全球的海洋科学进步和工程技术发展的贡献更大。为了深入了解留学生生活学习情况，编者在涉海类专业留学生中开展了"我们在浙大留学"主题征文活动，遴选和整理出近20个有代表性的在浙大留学的故事，集结出版。

本书以浙大涉海类专业留学生的视角，讲述他们在中国学习和生活的各种故事。这些故事内容丰富，形式多样，展示出留学生对中国历史文化和传统风俗的浓

---

① 原为国家海洋局第二海洋研究所，2018 年 3 月改为自然资源部第二海洋研究所。为全书统一，本书一律用现在的名称。

厚兴趣以及对中国先进科学技术的仰慕和赞叹，更有对校园生活和师生感情的难忘与不舍。

书中的每一段故事都讲述着来华留学生与中国、与浙大的相遇、相识与相知。在这些故事中，呈现着一张张真实、可爱的面容。有初来乍到的不适应，有对周围环境的陌生，有对语言不通的恐惧，有身在异乡的孤独……渐渐地，友善热情的浙大师生让他们感受到了家的温暖、兄弟姐妹般的关怀。了解中国文化，体验中国美食，开展科学研究，他们的中国留学之行收获颇丰。

透过文字，我们可以感受到留学生们在中国学习和生活的心路历程。他们潜心科研，奋发向上，把在中国学到的知识和先进的技术带回自己的祖国，成为国家的建设者、科技的领导者，成为中国与其他各国之间交流、合作的纽带。

国之交在于民亲，相信此书的出版不仅为留学生们记录了他们在中国、在浙大、在海洋二所的学习风采和生活感受，更是以"听世界讲中国"的方式给即将或未来赴中国留学的外国学生更多真实的参考，让他们对中国有更广泛的认识、更深层的了解。这将有助于弘扬和传播中国文化、揭示中国的发展理念、表达中国人民构建人类命运共同体的良好愿望，谋求开放创新、包容互惠的发展前景，促进和而不同、兼收并蓄的文明交流，构建尊崇自然、绿色发展的生态体系。

中国工程院院士、自然资源部第二海洋研究所所长

2018年9月于杭州

目 录
CONTENTS

缘于海上，成在浙里

2012年4月28日，执行大洋科考第26航次任务的中国"大洋一号"科考船从三亚起航。在38030海里、历时245天的航程中，"大洋一号"的旗帜飘过印度洋，飘过大西洋。大勇与中国情缘的故事，就从这里拉开了序幕。

扬帆起航：从尼日利亚到中国

在尼日利亚国家海洋研究所著名海洋地质学家、大陆架界限委员会主席阿沃西卡的邀请下，"大洋一号"航次专门为尼日利亚近海开展了为期半个月的科考。这次中尼联合调查航次，是我国首次在非洲国家专属经济区及其邻近海域开展的国际合作调查航次，被称为"中尼两国海洋科技合作的开创性之旅"。在双方的共同努力下，这次科研考察成功开展，不仅在尼日利亚西部大陆边缘获得了高精度地形地貌和地球物理场特征，填补了尼日利亚在此区域的海洋地质、地球物理调查空白，而且促进了中非海洋科技领域合作进入新阶段，加深了中尼双方的信任与情谊。大勇、Jimoh Olayinka Rasheed（中文名"军明"）、Akinnigbage Akintoye Edward（中文名"爱德华"）等尼日利亚国家海洋研究中心的科研人员，被安排参加了这次的科考任务。

大勇还有个更为有趣的身份，他是尼日利亚一个当地部落的酋长的儿子。刚到中国那会儿，大家都喊他"小王子"。"大勇"这个名字是后来老师为他取的，大勇特别喜欢这个中国名字。

大勇参加"大洋一号"航次科考,
左1为大勇
Dayong (left 1st) took part in
the ocean expedition of ship
Ocean One

大勇一行获得了海底下1.7米的样
品,右1为大勇
Dayong's (right 1st) team got
the sample of the 1.7m depth
under the sea

　　阿沃西卡与自然资源部第二海洋研究所(以下简称海洋二所)吕文正研究员同为大陆架委员成员,他多次访问海洋二所,对中国的海洋科研能力给予了非常高的评价。在访问海洋二所时他表示希望大勇等尼日利亚青年科学家能到中国来继续深造。

　　在为期半个月的合作科考中,大勇一行获得了海底下1.7米的珍贵样品。为了能在学术方面得到更高水平的指导,以及在更先进的科研条件下进行样品分析研究,他远渡重洋,携带样品从尼日利亚来到中国完成这次科考任务。

　　幸运总是不断降临在努力的人身上,此时恰逢中国政府设立海洋奖学金,专门为南海、太平洋和印度洋周边国家和地区及非洲的发展中国家的优秀青年来华攻读海洋及相关专业的硕士或博士学位提供资助。大勇格外珍惜中国的科研环境,在询问同伴的想法后,大勇、军明和爱德华三人不约而同希望能长期留在中国深造。他们申请到了中国政府的海洋奖学金，阿沃西卡的愿望也得到了实现。2013年9月，大勇有了新的身份——浙江大学首批招收的中国政府海洋奖学金学生，同时也是浙江大学海洋学院和海洋二所联合培养的博士生。在海洋二所招收的外籍学生里，大勇是第一个完成博士学位论文答辩的人。

瞭望前行：用五年时间换来的成长

当班机在杭州萧山机场降落时，大勇可能没想到，这一待就是五年。没有忐忑和担忧，大勇所携带的，除了珍贵的样品，就是求知欲和上进心。眼前的一切都极为新鲜，"世界上最美丽、优雅的城市杭州"、中国最好的大学之一……这一切都让大勇感到发自内心的兴奋。

在这里，大勇遇到了他的伯乐——浙江大学海洋学院的叶瑛教授和海洋二所的张海生研究员、陈建芳研究员。在大勇的心目中，叶瑛老师是个极为亲切的人，他如圭如璧，亦师亦亲，从科研到生活的方方面面都给予自己数不清的帮助。在大勇初到中国时，为了更好地帮助大勇融入中国的科研环境，叶瑛老师特意安排他跟随海洋学院邸雅楠老师学习，以便迅速适应。邸雅楠老师从事海洋生物的相关研究，曾留学英国。在邸老师的指导下大勇掌握了一系列海洋生物研究相关的技术和后期的数据统计方法，为以后的科研进一步夯实了根基。尽管师生二人相隔两地，不能时时见面，但提起叶瑛老师，大勇总是充满了敬意。从技能的基础学习，到研究的不断深入，直至博士学位论文的反复打磨，点点滴滴都凝聚着师生共同的汗水。

"大勇是个很上进的学生，"陈建芳老师脸上藏不住笑意，"每次参观学习总是他问题最多。"陈老师对大勇的学习非常重视，给予很大支持，特意安排了另外几位老师来对大勇的每项工作都进行具体的指导帮助。尽管平时科研工作繁忙，但无论线上还是线下，大勇的问题、疑难总是会被陈老师先行解决。大勇说这是自己的"特殊待遇"。在诸位老师的悉心指导和自己的努力下，大勇进步很快，崭露头角。他在第二届中国—东盟海洋科技论坛上作主题发言，参加欧盟组织的德国知名科考船"极星"（Polar Stern）号公开航次科考……目前，他已经发表了两篇论文，其中一篇发表在本学科领域的顶级SCI期刊上，该文的研究成果获得国内外同行的广泛引用，接下来还有两三篇科研成果即将发表。

大勇在第二届中国—东盟海洋科技论坛上作主题发言
Dayong made a presentation on the 2nd China–ASEAN Workshop on Marine Sciences and Technologies

大勇在博士阶段所做研究的主要方向就是对2012年科考中所获得的样品进行分析研究，他的博士学位论文也是就此展开的。海底下1.7米的地质样品，见证了几万年的变迁，承载了太多的历史，蕴含着无价的信息。尼日利亚作为非洲的第一人口大国，且地处沿海，正在迅速发展和进步之中，研究海洋地质和气候变迁记录对其整个国家的经济发展、国家安全都有着重要的意义。也正因此，大勇在学习科研中付出了更多，为自己，更为国家。

对大勇来说，中国与尼日利亚太不同了。浙江大学和海洋二所给予了他充足的支持，在极好的科研环境下、丰厚的学术氛围里，配以先进的仪器设备，他可以全心专注于自己的科研任务。如何获取和处理沉积物样品，挑选清洗后的有孔虫进行化学成分测试，如何操作诸如元素分析仪、气相色谱—质谱和超性能液相色谱—质谱等仪器，如何提取海洋生物的细胞样品并对其基因损伤进行测定……这些技能都是大勇通过在浙江大学和海洋二所的专业技术训练而掌握的。在这里，他从来都不缺乏与世界顶级学者交流学习的机会，单是每年上百场的学术讲座就足以让一个人成长的脚步从不停歇。这还得益于浙江大学的先进图书馆系统，即使身在中国，大勇也能够时刻关注国际前沿动态，获取第一手资源。他以前的同事不能有这样的机会，大勇为他们感到遗憾，也因此倍加珍惜现在的机会。随着科研水平的不断提高，大勇在尼日利亚国家海洋研究中心的职位已经从2013年刚来中国时的"Research Officer I"升为"Principal Research"，连升三级，他已成为该中心最年轻的首席科学家。

不觉归程：吹不散的情谊

如今已是大勇在中国的第五个年头，在对学位论文反复雕琢、精益求精的基础上，他成功地完成了博士论文答辩。大勇早已习惯了每天在紫金港校区和海洋二所之间往返的生活，在2018年3月底就要回到阔别已久的尼日利亚。而他对于自己已经生活了五年的中国，从初出国门时的一无所知到五年后的今天，已有了割舍不断的感情。

陈建芳研究员早年曾在德国工作学习，他深知在国外留学不仅仅是知识能力的提升，还有对当地文化的感悟吸收，在这期间建立的情谊即便随着时间的冲刷也是难以磨灭的。他鼓励大勇在科研之余多到外面走走看看，感受风土人情。大勇游过千岛湖的锦山秀水，看过青岛的碧海蓝天，到过历史悠久的金陵、和煦清新的厦门，走过巍峨万里的长城、雄伟大气的故宫，也曾赴京参加由中国国家海洋局主办的"蓝色梦想"

大勇代表留学生在中国政府海洋奖学金第一次游学活动中作报告
Dayong giving a speech on the first exchange programme of Marine Scholarship of China

中国政府海洋奖学金第一次游学活动，受到了国家海洋局陈连增副局长的亲切接见，并代表留学生对其在华留学期间的学习和研究进展作口头报告。

大勇的妻儿在浙大舟山校区（右3人为大勇一家）
Dayong's wife and child (right 1-3, Dayong's family) in Zhoushan campus of ZJU.

大勇热爱中国，喜欢中国生产的商品，使用的手机也是中国品牌小米。他会因为他人对中国的产品性价表示质疑而感到生气，甚至会与别人"argue"。因为他在中国，他知道真正的中国制造是什么样的。不仅是大勇，他的家人也对中国有着不一样的感情。大勇的妻子是当地医院里的护士，曾带孩子到杭州生活了3个月。回到尼日利亚后，每当看到中国人，她会情不自禁地感到亲切，唤出一声"你好"。

五年的时间，说长不长，说短不短，却足以成为一个人值得珍藏一生的回忆。大勇是一个怀揣梦想的年轻人，他远离故土，一往无前，在浙江大学和海洋二所共同搭建的舞台上尽情演绎了成长的乐章。是对科研、对国家的爱，陪他迈过坎坷，拥抱晴朗的天空。大勇希望回到尼日利亚后，尽己所能，将在中国学到的知识和技能传授给年轻的科学家和学生，为国家的发展做出更大的贡献，并继续作为联系中尼之间友谊的桥梁，致力于使两国科研人员彼此信任，携手共进。

采访人：张鸿乾

采访日期：2018年3月

大勇的妻儿路遇中国小朋友
Dayong's wife and child with a Chinese family on the street

From Ocean One to ZJU

On April 28, 2012, the Chinese science expedition ship Ocean One set sail from Sanya, China for her 26th voyage of mission. As she sailed over 38,030 nautical miles and spent 245 days across the Indian Ocean and the Atlantic Ocean, Dayong first started his China exploration.

Set sail: from Nigeria to China

Invited by Professor Awosika, a marine geologist in Nigerian Institute of Oceanography and Marine Research (NIOMR), the Chairman of the Committee of the Limits of the Continental Shelf (CLCS), Ocean One expedited at the Nigerian coast for half a month. As the first China-Africa joint ocean expedition in an African country's ocean economic zone, it was considered groundbreaking in Sino-Nigeria marine science and technology cooperation. The joint efforts made this mission a complete success. Not only did it figure out the high accuracy topography and the geophysical field characteristics of the continental margin along the west coast of Nigeria, making a new record in this field in this country, but also promoted the cooperation in marine science and technology into a new stage and deepened the mutual trust and friendship between China and Africa. Adedayo Adeleye (Chinese name "Dayong"), Jimoh Olayinka Rasheed (Chinese name "Junming"), Akinnigbage Akintoye Edward (Chinese name "Aidehua"), and many young researchers from NIOMR joined the expcdition.

Dayong's father is a tribe leader, namely Alaafin in Yorubaland, Nigeria. When he first came to China, he was called "little prince" before his Chinese teacher gave him the name Dayong, which means great and brave. He liked his Chinese name very much.

Professor Awosika and Dr. Lyu Wenzheng from the Second Institute of Oceanography (SIO), Ministry of Natural Resources of China, both work as committee members of the CLCS. After visiting SIO a few times, Professor Awosika highly evaluated the Chinese marine research capabilities. He showed great expectations for having young Nigeria scientists to China for their further study.

In the half-month cooperative research, Dayong and his colleagues obtained a precious sample of the 1.7m depth under the sea. In order to get a better academic guidance and a more advanced scientific research condition for the sample analysis, Dayong travelled with the

sample from Nigeria all the way to China.

Good luck falls only on those who are ready for it. Coincidently, a new scholarship was offered by the Chinese government to the outstanding young oceanography scientists from the countries and regions of the South China Sea, the Pacific and the Indian Ocean and from the developing countries in Africa, especially for their diploma study of a master's or a doctoral degree in marine science and technology. It was a great opportunity for Dayong and his colleagues, and for fulfilling Professor Awosika's dream as well. In September, 2013, Dayong was fortunate to be one of the first China's marine scholarship awardees enrolled by Zhejiang University (ZJU), and the first international PhD candidate jointly instructed by the ZJU Ocean College and SIO. Among all the international students at SIO, Dayong was the first to finish his Doctorate degree dissertation and graduated from the program.

Look ahead: Growth in the five years

When his plane landed at Hangzhou Xiaoshan international airport, Dayong may have never thought about staying 5 years in China. Without any fear or worries, Dayong only had his inquisitiveness and initiatives along with the precious sediment samples for his research. Everything was so new to him—the top-notch University in China, the beautiful city. He was excited about his new life.

Dayong was lucky to have a group of helpful professors—Professor Ye Ying (ZJU), Dr. Zhang Haisheng (SIO), and Dr. Chen Jianfang (SIO), etc. Dr. Ye was so kind and helpful that Dayong did not only take him as a good instructor and supervisor but also a family-like friend. When he first arrived, Prof. Ye had Dr. Di Ya'nan from SIO help him fit into the team as soon as possible. Dr. Di studied marine biology in the United Kingdom. With her help, Dayong learnt a lot of the research techniques in marine biology and in the statistical analysis, forming a solid foundation for his later study. Although Dayong and Professor Ye lived in two different cities and couldn't meet each other frequently, Dayong was all respect talking about Professor Ye. He could never forget about Professor Ye's great efforts throughout his PhD study. From fundamental techniques to profound theories and to his doctoral dissertation, Professor Ye went through every detail with him.

"Dayong is well initiated, " said Dr. Chen Jianfang, a professor from SIO, one of Dayong's instructors, "He was the most inquisitive in field studies." Dr. Chen was all smiles talking about Dayong. Although being busy all the time, Dr. Chen paid a lot of attention to

Dayong and gave him great supports. He even managed to have several other researchers to give specific guidance in his study. Hence, Dr. Chen was always the first one from whom Dayong would seek for help online or offline. He said this was a "special favor" to him. With the help of the researchers at the ZJU Ocean College and SIO, Dayong made such rapid progresses that he soon extinguished himself from his peers. He made a presentation on the 2nd China-ASEAN Workshop on Marine Sciences and Technologies; he went to the expedition trip organized by the European Union on the Polar Stern, the well-known German science expedition ship. Upon the interview, he had published two papers, one of which was widely cited and was published in a top SCI journal. He also had another 2-3 under reviewing before publication.

Dayong analyzed the samples he obtained from the expedition in 2012 for his PhD dissertation. The 1.7 meters of geological sample dug out from the ocean bottom witnessed the changes in this area in the tens of thousands of years, bearing so much priceless historical information. As the most populous country in Africa, Nigeria is located in the West African coast. The study of marine geology and climate change means a lot to the country's rapid economic development and national security.

China and Nigeria are extremely different to Dayong. ZJU and SIO gave him plenty of support. In the pleasant research environment and the dynamic academic atmosphere, with the advanced instruments and equipments, he was able to focus on his research. He had learnt to subsample the core sediment at an interval, to pick and clean up the foraminifera tests, to freeze the dried sediment, to extract and purify the cell samples of marine organisms in order to test the genetic damages caused by pollution, and to operate such instruments as elemental analyzer, gas chromatography mass spectrometry, and super functional liquid chromatography mass spectrometry. He had the opportunity to learn from the world's leading scholars about the forefront knowledge in his major via the hundreds of academic lectures year round. Thanks to the advanced library system of ZJU and SIO, he had an access to the cutting-edge discoveries in the world and the first-hand resources. Dayong felt regretful for his former colleagues who had no access to such a resource and treasured his stay in China. With the constant improvement of his scientific research skills, Dayong was promoted from the "Research Officer" in 2013 when he first got there to the present "Principal Researcher", becoming the youngest principal researcher in his institute back in Nigeria.

Time to return: Friendship forever

It is the fifth year of Dayong's stay in China. After the repeated revising and polishing, he finished his doctoral degree dissertation and passed the defense. Back in Nigeria in late March, he developed a sentimental feeling for China and for ZJU, as he had been so used to commuting between Zijingang Campus and SIO in the past few years.

Dr. Chen Jianfang who used to study and work in Germany knows that studying abroad does not only mean learning in classes but also means experiencing the culture and building up friendships. With his encouragement, Dayong explored the community to experience the local custom. Dayong had been to different places, such as the Thousand-Island Lake in Chun'an, Zhejiang Province, Qingdao in Shandong Province, Nanjing in Jiangsu Province, and Xiamen in Fujian Province. As one of the awardees of the marine scholarship, he had been to Beijing for a trip sponsored by Ministry of Natural Resources of China, visiting the Great Wall, Tiananmen Square and the Forbidden City. During the trip, he met the deputy director of SOA, Mr. Chen Lianzeng and made a speech on behalf of the international students.

Dayong loved China and the things made in China. He would be irritated if anyone questioned the cost-effectiveness of the things made in China and would even argue with him or her. He thought that he had a say in terms of the virtual Made-in-China, as he lived here. Because of him, his family also developed a special love for China. His wife, a nurse in St. Nicholas Hospital in Lagos, Nigeria, lived in Hangzhou for three months, along with their child. After she went back to Nigeria, she couldn't help having a close feeling for the Chinese there and would greet them with "Nihao. "

Five years was not too long, nor too short. It was enough to make unforgettable memories in one's lifetime. Dayong came with a dream and worked hard for it. With the supports from both ZJU and SIO, he had performed very well in his studies. His passion for the scientific research and his love for his country were the dynamic for him to overcome the difficulties and to succeed. After his return Dayong hoped to teach the young researchers and students what he had learnt in China to make greater contributions to his country and to bridging China and Nigeria.

Postscript: Upon the first meeting with Dayong, it was not hard to detect his passion. A simple greeting of "Nihao" of his from 50 meters away quickly drew me closer to him. Before taking a seat, he had made tea for me. During the interview, Dayong kept refilling the tea to keep it warm—a well-performed Chinese etiquette. Dr. Chen Jianfang managed to spare the whole afternoon from his hustles and bustles to translate during the interview. I acknowledge my thanks here.

学以致用，船渡重洋

    电脑屏幕透出微微的光，Arfish Maydino（斐谞）独自专注地看着屏幕上的仿真模型，在光标游走间不断进行着调整与运算。为了能完成好手上的任务，像这样的工作，他已经在实习企业连续干了几个月；进入企业以来，斐谞切切实实地感受到在企业实习与在学校学习的异同。

斐谞(左1)在浙江大学学习期间参加导师课题组组会
Arfish (left 1st) in a meeting of his research group at Zhejiang University

    对这位印度尼西亚籍的浙江大学留学生Arfish Maydino，大家总亲切地叫他斐谞，一个很有中国文化韵味的名字。2014年9月，在中国政府海洋奖学金的支持下，斐谙停止了他在印度尼西亚技术评估应用处（Agency for the Assessment and Application of Technology）的工作，来到浙江大学攻读硕士学位。在此期间，他的研究方向是船舶设计和流体动力学（ship design and hydrodynamics），其中主要是流体动力学的相关计算（CFD）。经过一年的学习与积淀，斐谙的理论功底和研发能力都得到了极大的提升。为了更好地锻炼斐谙的知识运用能力，2015年9月他的导师冷建兴教授安排他进入浙江大学海洋学院研究生实习基地——杭州华鹰游艇有限公司（Sino Eagle Shipyard）实习。留学生进入中国民营企业的情况并不多见，但这丝毫不影响斐谙的融入感。企业安排斐谙参与了当时公司正在研发的双体水翼游艇项目，并让他负责该研发项目的总体性能优化设计工作。

杭州华鹰游艇有限公司位于杭州西南部的富阳东洲岛，与浙江大学建立了长期的校企合作的联盟，公司产品均远销海外。富春江畔，江洲鹭影。相比繁华的杭州，富阳少了几分喧嚣，多了几分宁静。不同的生活环境，加之企业实习有别于校园学习的特殊性，在富阳度过的这十个月让斐谙十分难忘。

斐谙在杭州华鹰游艇有限公司实习时和企业内部的技术人员一起工作
Working with the technicians at Sino Eagle Shipyard

尽管开始实习前斐谙已经在中国学习了一年，但他的汉语水平仍不足以应对骤然改变的环境以及工作中急剧增加的沟通交流。而且，富阳当地居民与企业内部熟知英文的员工也不多，这让他在面对语言方面的阻力时常感到不知所措。然而也正是这份压力促成了斐谙在汉语语言听说方面的飞速进步。在实习过程中，游艇公司的技术人员基本用中文和斐谙进行交流，他的导师冷教授也时常提醒斐谙要再多学些中文。因此斐谙时常会找一些中文书籍来读，还给自己定了个小目标：每天学会10个中文词语。经过长达半年的积累，他用中文交流的能力已经有了明显的进步，口音也变得地道起来。在他的朋友圈中，亲人和朋友们常能看到他用中文记录的日记，分享他在中国科研实习的点点滴滴、酸甜苦辣。

斐谞不仅在语言方面投入精力，在参与的项目研发工作中更是全力以赴。杭州华鹰游艇有限公司正在研发的是高速双体水翼游艇，这种游艇兼具了双体船和水翼艇的优点，既有双体船的高稳定性，又有水翼艇的超低船舶阻力的特点，体现了近年来船舶技术发展的趋势。在该项目研发过程中，斐谞分担了水翼艇静水力计算、翼航稳定性计算以及国外水翼艇资料收集等工作，同时还参与了水翼的攻角调整、水翼艇航行试验等实际工作。他通过理论计算和CFD方法进行仿真模拟，将模拟结果与方案设计结果进行比对，并提出了改进建议。经过彼此间长期的沟通交流，第一艘双体水翼船终于在团队的共同努力下完成建造。虽然所有人都对游艇的表现满怀期待，却还是发现了问题——游艇速度上不去，而这就意味着游艇尚未达到设计目标。

面对问题，迎难而上。这次不理想的试验激励着斐谞多学多练，将所学知识应用到实处。经过斐谞与公司设计人员的共同努力，改进后的游艇再次下水，试验结果通过与CFD模拟进行比较得到验证，并且相互之间表现出高度一致性，象征着一种新型的高速双体水翼游艇已经诞生。

然而，斐谞所完成的还不止于此。他在出色完成双体水翼游艇项目工作的同时，还在出口澳大利亚游艇的项目中，承担了倾斜试验大纲编制、稳性计算等工作，并始终与公司研发人员保持紧密合作，助力项目推进。通过团队合作，斐谞全方位的技术和管理能力都得到了提升。尤其在项目的实艇航行试验阶段，他对团队的研究结果和设计结果进行了全方位的测试和验证，试验结果又可以为后续的优化设计提供依据。在公司实习期间，斐谞在船舶设计和性能研究方面得到了全方位的提高。

刚到富阳开始实习时，斐谞还有些许的不适应与犹豫，但经过了一段时间充实和快节奏的实习，他的优异表现得到了实习企业和导师的一致好评，这也让他更具自信。斐谞坦言道，在学校中自己学到了扎实的理论基础，实习把自

斐谞一家三口在富阳生活
Arfish's family in Fuyang

己在学校所学到的理论付诸实践，在这个过程中还要尽力解决一些如沟通交流等的实际工作困难，这对自身知识增长和能力提高都很有好处，也让自己取得了更多的收获。

当然，斐谞也不是一个人在奋斗，无论是在浙江大学，还是在实习企业，他的家人都陪伴在旁，这让斐谞对中国产生了更强的第二故乡情怀。

自斐谞开始实习以来，他的妻子和儿子就来到了富阳，并一直陪着他到毕业回国。对这难得聚在一起的一家人，杭州华鹰游艇有限公司人性化地为他们提供温馨的生活条件，提供免费的住宿与伙食，每月还给斐谞发放2000元的生活补贴，再加上中国政府发给的每月3000元的生活费，确保其能够安心参与一线的科研生产。在他们所居住的那片地方，斐谞一家是唯一的外国家庭，因此邻里对他们都格外照顾。时至今日，斐谞的妻子还会常常怀念在中国生活的日子，怀念相处极好、多有照扶的邻里，她也期盼着能再回来看看这片生活了一年多的土地。

对斐谞来说，怀念的则不仅仅是在中国这第二故乡的温馨生活，更有导师冷教授的严谨指导。在他心目中，冷教授对自己的帮助一直是润物细无声的，无论是在学术还是非学术问题上，无论是对其个人还是家庭上，冷教授都给予了他超出导师职责本身的诸多帮扶。就学术而言，冷教授为斐谞制定了合适的研修规划和课题实施计划，在恰当的时候他总会提出建议和意见，保证斐谞在每一个阶段都能够获得成功。这既鼓舞了他深入研究下去，又能够在发现问题时及时纠正。在浙大求学期间，斐谞发表了一篇期刊论文和一篇会议论文。他

导师推荐斐谞参加第二届中国—东盟海洋
科技学术研讨会
Professor Leng recommended Arfish to
the Second China-ASEAN Workshop
on Ocean Science and Technology

很感激冷教授给自己的学习与科研过程保留了许多独立的空间，让他从中学到
了独立行事的能力，这将使他受益终生。

　　时间一晃，到了2017年3月，斐谞顺利通过了硕士学位论文答辩。他又
回到了杭州，在紫金港校区的体育馆里参加了学位授予仪式和毕业典礼。那天
他舒畅地大笑，高兴地把学位证书捧在身前，在会场上和朋友、家人合影留
念。他们的身后，"梦起浙大，难说再见"八个大字，格外醒目。两年半的求
学经历，像倍速的电影般在眼前掠过：同学亲洽、师生和睦、参加学校晚会演

斐谞（前排右3）在浙江大学学位授予仪式上
Arfish at the Zhejiang University Degree Awarding Ceremony（front row right 3）

出、和海洋学院足球队一同踢球、实习、与家人重聚、攻克技术难关、发表论文……

　　现在，斐谞已经和家人返回印度尼西亚。斐谞重新回到了印度尼西亚国家海洋技术中心技术评估应用处工作。在两年半的中国学习期间，他的科研能力获得了全方位的提升。正如"能力越大，责任越大"所述，工作中离不开他的地方愈发多了，他的工作也愈发繁忙了。人生并非一直是漫天灿烂的星空，可对斐谞而言，在浙大求学的经历必然是其中耀眼璀璨的一颗明星，在斐谞的眼里熠熠生辉。

　　"在过去的几年中，感谢有你们！"

斐谞学成回国工作
Arfish back to work in Indonesia

采访人：张鸿乾

采访日期：2018年9月

Sail Across the Ocean to Learn and to Practice

In the dim light of his computer screen, Arfish Maydino stared at the simulation model he made, punching in some words once in a while as the cursor moved about on the screen. In order to complete the task at hand, he has been worked like this as an intern for several months. After entering the company, Arfish Maydino has found the similarities and differences between an internship and school learning.

Arfish Maydino has a very Chinese nickname Fei Xu. In September 2014, with the support of the Marine Scholarship of China, Arfish quit his work at the Agency for the Assessment and Application of Technology in Indonesia and came to Zhejiang University to pursue a master's degree, studying Ship Design and Hydrodynamics, mainly the related calculations of fluid dynamics (CFD). After a year of study, Arfish made a great progess in both theory learning and research competence. In order to have Arfish apply his knowledge, in September 2015, his instructor, Professor Leng Jianxing arranged for him to be an intern at Sino Eagle Shipyard, a postgraduate internship base of Zhejiang University Ocean University. Not many international students work in a Chinese private enterprise, but Arfish integrated well. The company had him join the twin-body hydrofoil yacht designing program, and asked him to be in charge of the optimization of its overall performance.

Sino Eagle Shipyard company is located in Fuyang Dongzhou Island, a southwestern suburb of Hangzhou. The company has established a long-term cooperation with Zhejiang University. Its products have a good export record. Compared to the city noise in Hangzhou, Fuyang is somewhat less crowded and more quiet. The blurry and foggy Fuchun river and the herons flying over it make up a different living environment, not to mention that being an intern in a corporate is very different from the learning on campus. The ten months in Fuyang were unforgettable to Arfish.

Although Arfish had studied in China for a year before having this internship, his Chinese was not competent enough to cope with the rapid change of environment and the drastic increase in communication at work. Plus, few local residents and employees in Fuyang knew English. He was overwhelmed and frustrated by the language barrier. However, his listening and speaking capabilities boomed with such exposure. During the internship, the technicians communicated with Arfish mostly in Chinese, and his instructor, Professor Leng, often encouraged him to learn Chinese. Arfish found some Chinese books to read, setting a goal for himself: learn ten Chinese words every day. In half a year, his Chinese became fluent, even his accent became localized. In his WeChat moments, he even wrote diaries in Chinese, sharing every bitterness and happiness in his daily life as an intern.

Arfish was not only committed to language learning, but also devoted to his work. What Sino Eagle Shipyard was designing was a high-speed twin-body hydrofoil yacht, which combines the merits of catamaran and hydrofoil—being as stable as catamarans and with a super low resistance like a hydrofoil. It goes with the general trend of ship development in recent years. Arfish's work was to calculate hydrostatic force of hydrofoil, the wing stability, to collect reference of hydrofoils worldwide, and to adjust the hydrofoil attack angle for the navigation tests. He made the simulation via theoretical calculation and CFD method, comparing it with the schemes of design so as to give proposals for improvement. After all the communications and the joint efforts of the team, the first twin-body hydrofoil was finally built. Despite of all the expectations for it, the yacht failed to speed up, which means that it was not so good as it was supposed.

Faced with the problem and the challenge, Arfish was initiated to learn better and apply what he learned to practice. Arfish joined the other designers to improve the yacht until it was launched again. The test results were verified by the CFD simulations and showed a high degree of consistency. This was a landmark achievement that a new type of high-speed twin-body hydrofoil yacht was born.

What Arfish has done is far more than this. While fulfilling the double-body hydrofoil yacht project, he also undertook the preparation for the tilting tests and the stability calculation in making the yachts to be exported to Australia. He always maintained close cooperation with the company's researchers to help promote the project. Through such teamwork, Arfish had made a big progress in terms of comprehensive technical and management competence; especially during the actual ship navigation test, he made an omni comprehensive test and verification of the team's research results and design results, and in turn, provides data for the following optimization designing. During his internship at the company, Arfish has been fully improved in ship design and performance research.

When he first got to Fuyang for his internship, Arfish was uncomfortable and hesitant. After a period of learning and the fast-paced internship, his excellent performance was highly praised by the intern companies and his professors. This made him more confident. Arfish admits that the internship helped applying the theories that he had learned in school into practice. In addition, from all his efforts on overcoming difficulties such as communication, he was benefited both in knowledge and in capabilities.

Of course, Arfish is not alone, whether at Zhejiang University, or in the internship company, he has always been companied by his family, which makes Arfish develop a strong feelings for China as his second hometown.

His wife and his son went to Fuyang with him from the very beginning of his internship till his graduation and returned home with him. For this family who overcame so many difficulties to get together, Sino Eagle Shipyard company provided them with a good living condition, free accommodations and meals, and a monthly living allowance of 2,000 yuan. Taking into account the 3,000 yuan monthly living allowance supplied by the Chinese government scholarship, Arfish had no worries for living. That ensured his commitment to the scientific research and production. In the place where they lived, Arfish's family was the only foreigners. The neighbors took good care of them. Even up to now, Arfish's wife would often miss the days of living in China and miss her kind neighbors. She hoped to come back to the place where she lived for more than a year.

Arfish does not only miss the life in his second hometown—China, but also the rigorous guidance of Professor Leng. In his mind, Professor Leng's help to him was as penetrating as the spring rain, whether it was on academic or non-academic issues, whether it was for him or for his family, Professor Leng had given a lot of help, some of which was even beyond an instructor's duties. Academically, Professor Leng worked out a suitable training plan and project implementation plan for Arfish, giving him suggestions and opinions at the key points to ensure his success at every stage. This encouraged him to study further and to readjust himself in time if there were any problems. During his stay at Zhejiang University, Arfish published an article on a journal and a paper on a conference. He is very grateful to Professor Leng for retaining a lot of independent space in his study and research process, so that he can learn to be independent and can be benefited from it for life.

Time flies. In March 2017, Arfish successfully passed the master's thesis defense. He returned to Hangzhou and attended the degree awarding ceremony and the commencement at the stadium of Zijin'gang Campus. On that day, he laughed comfortably and happily, holding the degree certificate in front of him, taking photos with his friends and family at the venue. Behind them, the eight characters of "Dream started from Zheda(ZJU). It's hard to depart", which was particularly eye-catching. The two and a half years of study flashed by like a speed movie in his mind—his classmates and teachers, the school evening performances, the Ocean

College football team, his internships, the reunion with his family, the moments of overcoming technology difficulties, publishing articles...

Arfish has returned to Indonesia with his family, resuming his work at the Agency for the Assessment and Application of Technology. As his research ability has been improved in all aspects, he has to take on more work responsibilities and becomes busier and busier. As it is often said "The greater the ability, the greater the responsibility." Life is not always a starry sky. But for Arfish, his life at Zhejiang University is bound to be a shining star in his eyes whenever he looks at it.

"Thank you for the past few years," as he would often say.

为了故乡的那一轮明月

暂别故土，逐梦中国

法罕的中国求学之旅，要从他的博士梦说起。

从故乡巴基斯坦的白沙瓦大学国家地质卓越中心取得了地质学硕士学位后，法罕担任过研究助理，不久后到了阿富汗，在阿玛尼亚矿业公司担任地质学家一职，并工作了三年。纵然早已步入工作岗位，法罕的内心深处对学习的渴望之火却始终没有熄灭。对他而言，继续接受教育绝对是一个不二之选，而他希望深层次研究的领域——地质学，则更是他的热情所在。所以，当他获得中国政府海洋奖学金而能来中国深造时，他觉得已经踏上了实现梦想的第一步。更让他惊喜的是，他要就读的大学是中国最好的大学之一的浙江大学。

报名阶段他向叶瑛教授提交了自己的申请材料和研究设想。扎实的专业背景、丰富的工作经验，还有清晰的研究思路得到了导师的充分肯定，法罕如愿以偿收到了浙江大学的录取通知书。当梦想的轮廓逐渐清晰，他有了更具体的目标：不仅要获得浙江大学的博士学位，还要为家乡矿业资源的开发和经济腾飞做出贡献。

2016年9月，法罕终于踏上了中国的土地。他首先到达美丽的杭州，就学于浙江大学海洋学院。一年后，他随导师到了舟山校区，开始新的学习与生活。

杭州和舟山，在法罕眼里就像是中国大家庭里的两位名媛。古城杭州不仅有秀丽的风光，被誉为人间天堂，更有丰富的历史文化底蕴，号称六朝古都。

这里还是中国的电子商务和移动支付的摇篮，孕育了阿里巴巴这个电子商务和移动支付的国际知名企业。

如果说杭州是富丽堂皇的名门闺秀，舟山则像是深藏不露的小家碧玉。浙江大学舟山校区坐落在东海之滨，依山傍水，气候宜人。那里少了大城市的喧嚣，散发出宁静、平和的气质，这恰恰与法罕专注沉稳的性格契合，使他的心灵因为与环境的默契而透露出希望的光辉。可以呼吸到清新无污染的空气，培养起十分沉静的心态，法罕说，这里是潜心修学的好地方。

地球科学的奥秘不仅在书本中、在课堂上，更在自然山水间。法罕在闲暇时也注重观察杭州、舟山和他游览的名山大川中的地质现象。对这么一个热爱地质学的学生来说，中国的层峦叠嶂、江河湖海，森林草原，多种多样又具有地域特色的自然景观，实在是太吸引人了。同时，他也对舟山跨海大桥等工程抱有极大的兴趣。他目光所到处，大自然的鬼斧神工和建设者们的智慧力量在科学的殿堂交相辉映。法罕对自己专业的热爱已经上升到了悟道者的高度。

患难真情，浙里有"家"

留学意味着告别故土，告别亲人，这并不是一件轻松的事，新婚仅五天便要飞去中国的法罕对此深有体会。当然有激动，当然有憧憬，但在离别的那时刻，内心充斥的，却是依恋与不舍。离愁别绪让这个新郎感到了"生活不仅有快乐的一面，也有悲伤的一面"，他永远不会忘记离开家人时的感受。

不过，这样的情感没有过度地延续，法罕是非常幸运的——在到达中国两个月后，法罕的妻子也成功申请到了浙江大学海洋学院的硕士学位攻读资格，来到了浙江大学舟山校区。于是，新婚夫妇便得以一起学习、生活，彼此陪伴。

不久，法罕的妻子怀孕了。他们非常开心。孕期开始时，一切都非常顺利。可将为人父人母的他们却万万没有想到，在一次例行检查后，医生告诉法罕夫妇，婴儿的健康受到了极大的威胁，实际上没有呼吸。问题还不仅在胎儿，法罕妻子自身的健康也处在危险状态，她的血管中存在血栓，并且有凝血倾向。这是一种原因不明的罕见疾病，如果血栓靠近心、肺、脑等重要器官，就会危及生命。妊娠期并发血栓使得问题更加棘手，抗凝血药物很有可能造成大量失血。法罕夫妇深知问题的严重性，毕竟，在法罕妻子的族人中，已经有好几位被无情的血栓夺去了宝贵的生命。这一疾病是具有家族倾向性的。

妻子的健康到了危险关头。是回国治疗，还是在中国就医？小两口面临艰难的选择。最终，出于对中国医生、中国医院的高度信任，他们决定在浙江大学附属第一医院就医。

法罕的妻子在浙医一院做了流产，并在医院接受了较长时间的住院治疗。明智的决定与有效的治疗最终使法罕的妻子恢复了健康。回想起来，他们经历了异常艰难的阶段，在此期间，担心、难过、忐忑等情绪反反复复地敲击着法罕的心。第一次经历这样的事，而且还是在异国他乡——在中国，而非自己的祖国，法罕觉得这一切是那么难以忘记。这是留学生活中重重的一抹印记。他永远不会忘记，中国医院的救死扶伤简直像疾风一样迅速，从接诊、住院、分析诊断到确诊治疗，整个过程一气呵成，片刻也没有耽搁。在妻子住院期间，医生、护士都给予了无微不至的关怀，积极帮助病人渡过难关。价格不菲的医疗费用得到了学校、医院的资助和减免，也得到了很多相识和不相识的中国朋友与国际友人的支持，法罕夫妇对这一切都心存感激。得益于中国医生的高超医术和社会各界的关爱，他妻子很快恢复了健康，他们又能在浙江大学的校园里比翼双飞了。

除了妻子的陪伴，法罕还结交了不少中国朋友。在课余时间里，丰富的校园活动给了法罕休闲娱乐与了解中国的机会。他在朋友的教授下学会了打羽毛球，也爱上了这门运动，他和朋友参加了海洋学院举行的羽毛球比赛，并且拿到了男子双打冠军的好成绩。从不知怎么持羽毛球拍到成为冠军，法罕对此非常惊喜。他受到鼓励，还挑战自己，在新年晚会上唱了一首歌，大家的赞赏至今还让他欣喜不已。

在与中国老师、朋友的相处中，法罕对中国人有了了解。在他眼里，中国人勤劳、真诚、善良。"世界上有这么多人，每个人都有自己的经验和思维方式"，而法罕体会到了中国人的热情与善意。

2017年1月至2月，海洋学院的所有留学生都在位于杭州的浙江大学玉泉校

法罕在新年晚会上的精彩表演
The excellent performance of Farhan on New Year's party

区过春节。法罕对春节举行的活动非常感兴趣，他开始了解中国的节日。在中国调查的课程作业中，法罕做了关于红包的介绍展示，受到了老师的赞赏。这对他来说是一个有趣的话题，因为在他的祖国巴基斯坦的文化中，人们在古尔邦节上也有类似红包的"Eidi"。

在中国生活了近两年，法罕学到的不仅仅是专业的知识，还有对生活在异国他乡的体验与对中国文化的感知。去过了风景秀美而繁华热闹的杭州，游览过了"东海明珠"普陀，他还希望能参观北京、上海等中国城市，这也是他"学习之旅"的一部分。法罕对中国怀抱着的爱，不仅仅是因为他来自中国的友好邻邦。在巴基斯坦，中巴友谊早已深入人心，而他与中国的情谊就像是中巴关系的小小缩影。他们夫妇在中国的留学经历，将成为伴随他们一生的精神财富。

笃定信念，勇攀高峰

法罕和导师合作的研究课题，是研究巴基斯坦北部中巴边境地区的金矿成矿作用，研究在这一地区形成大型、超大型金矿的可能性。

选择这样一个课题，他和他的导师叶瑛教授可以说是英雄所见略同。在入学前，法罕在这一地区已从事了好几年的野外地质和找矿勘探工作。他最初提交的研究方案针对的是巴基斯坦北部高原的沙金矿床。在与导师讨论、切磋后，他将研究重点转移到了沙金的源头，即内生岩金矿床上。

巴基斯坦不缺少星星，但是月亮在哪里？这是导师给他的第一个思考题。叶瑛教授把当地的沙金矿称为星星，把岩金矿比作月亮。这一比喻很形象，也恰如其分。巴北山区几乎每一条溪流、河道中都有沙金分布，星罗棋布，但规模较小。当地人在溪流中淘金足以温饱，但很难形成工业化开采，也难以支撑社会经济发展。另一方面，在与巴基斯坦北部高原毗邻的地区，从西部的吉尔吉斯斯坦、阿富汗，到中国的西藏，乃至东面的缅甸，大型铜、金矿床比比皆是，这些矿床和巴基斯坦北部高原属于同一构造带，应该有类似的成矿条件。数星星不如赏月亮，法罕采纳了导师的建议。

"我们的研究不仅要有理论成果，更要关注它对社会经济发展的影响。"这是导师对所有学生常说的话。在学生们的眼中，他们的老师是个"画饼大师"——擅长把枯燥、深奥的科学目标描绘成香喷喷的大饼，目前它还在墙上，只要你如何如何去努力，这大饼就会落在你的盘子里。这葵花宝典自然也

法罕（左）与导师叶瑛教授在一起
Farhan (left) with his instructor Professor Ye Ying

用在了法罕头上。法罕并不觉得导师画在墙上的大饼是遥不可及的，毕竟满天星斗预示着总有一天会众星拱月，既然那一轮明月已经照亮了邻国，那为何不会照亮克什米尔高原呢？这里作为中巴经济走廊的必经之路，将有一条高速公路和铁路连接新疆喀什和巴基斯坦的瓜达尔港，配套的大型水电、火电等基础设施也在建设中。如果地质学家在金矿地质勘探、成矿理论上取得进展，将会迅速转变成经济效益和社会效益，国运、家运都会走上发展的快车道。

当然，实现这一目标真的不容易，要知道，在克什米尔开展过地质勘探工作的不仅有巴基斯坦当地企业，还有众多的国外矿产公司，不乏装备精良、经验丰富的高手。但是这里的自然条件难比平原地区。离开了山谷和溪流，就是"交通靠走、通讯靠吼"的原生态环境。

2017年的暑假前，导师叶瑛教授和法罕一起拟订了一个野外工作计划。潜在的矿化分明是在崇山峻岭中，有些地段甚至靠近了当地雪线。"我腿脚不便，这野外工作就靠你了，"导师拍着法罕的肩膀说。他没去过巴基斯坦，但十来年前去过昆仑山脉的另一面，也就是新疆境内的帕米尔高原，那里山势海拔都不亚于克什米尔。好汉不提当年勇，毕竟年纪不饶人。年轻的法罕便带着导师的期待与探索的热情走进了野外。

三个月后，也就是十月中旬，法罕从克什米尔带回了上百千克的样品。

不知道他是骑毛驴进去的，还是坐驴车进去的。导师或许心里在想，但并没有这么问，一切的艰辛都写在了法罕的脸上。他黑里透红的肤色分明就是这几个月风餐露宿的印记，那双明眸中闪烁着的光亮，向导师述说着他带回的是家乡人民的希望。接下来的工作同样不轻松，为了墙上那张大饼，还有自己的国运、家运，法罕可是拼了。"愿安拉保佑法罕"，导师常把这句话挂在嘴边。

在浙江大学舟山校区的海洋学院里，一位负责敬业的好导师带领着信念笃定的好学生，守护着一个梦，这就是法罕的梦。法罕的梦，就是能接受良好的教育，获得博士学位，为家乡矿床资源的开发和经济腾飞做出贡献。

这是一个地质学家报国的梦，富国的梦，也是法罕自己人生中最珍贵的初心。无论前路还有多少挑战，法罕在中国的追梦之旅都会继续下去，他和导师都相信，总有一天，从"浙里"出发的梦将会实现——"那轮明月"将会照亮克什米尔高原，经济腾飞，家国兴旺，巴基斯坦人民将在那月光下伴着手鼓和吉他起舞，庆祝越来越美好的生活。

法罕在克什米尔进行地质勘探和采样
Farhan in the geological exploring and sampling at Kashmir

采访人：张明珉

采访日期：2018年3月

All for My Hometown

Leaving home for China to pursue my dream

Farhan's journey to China started from his dream of being a doctor.

After getting his master's degree from the National Centre of Excellence in Geology, University of Peshawar in Pakistan, Farhan first worked as a research assistant. Then he went to Afghanistan working in Amania Mining Company for three years. In those years, Farhan kept his zeal for learning, especially for a further education in geology. Therefore, when he was awarded the Marine Scholarship of China to study in the doctorate program in Zhejiang University, he had a sense of setting off for his dream. He was even more surprised learning that ZJU was one of the top universities in China.

Along with his application, Farhan submitted his research proposal to professor Ye Ying. With his profound professional background, rich work experience, and clear research plan, his proposal was accepted by professor Ye. After being admitted by ZJU, his dream became clearer, his target became more specific—besides obtaining his doctorate degree, he would work for the mining and the economic development of his country.

In September 2016, Farhan arrived in Hangzhou, first settled down in the Ocean College of the University. A year later, he moved to the ZJU Zhoushan campus with his professor for the second phase of his study.

Hangzhou and Zhoushan are both charming to Farhan. Named as "Paradise on Earth", Hangzhou is not only beautiful but also Known for its history and Culture. In history, the city used to be the capital for six dynasties; while in the modern time, Hangzhou is home to Alibaba, the e-commerce and mobile payment giant known in China and in the world.

If Hangzhou can be compared to a noble lady, Zhoushan is more like a neighboring girl with implicit beauty. The ZJU Zhoushan campus is located on the east coast of the island. Surrounded by hills and water, it has a wonderful climate throughout the year. Without the hustles and bustles of big cities, Zhoushan is so quiet and peaceful, so fresh and clean that it goes perfectly with Farhan's dedication and concentration. Farhan said it was soul making and inspiring.

The mysteries of earth science are not taught in books and courses, but in nature. In his spare time, Farhan explored the geological phenomena in Hangzhou, Zhoushan, and other famous mountains and rivers he had visited. As a student, he was not only so keen on geology, the natural landscapes, say, the mountains, rivers, lakes, forests, and grasslands, but also had great interests in the cross-sea bridge, especially the cross-ocean bridges in Zhoushan. Both the power of nature and the intelligence of man inspired him so much that his passion for his study was raised to a philosophical height.

Love and support from ZJU in his difficult time

Studying abroad is never easy. It means to leave one's home and family. Farhan flew to China on the 5th day after his wedding. It was not hard to imagine how reluctant he was at the moment of departure, even though he was excited by his enrollment. As Farhan said he would never forget the complex sensation when saying good-bye to his bride. It was so real to him that happy time ended fast.

However, the sore did not last very long. Farhan's wife also got an offer from the ZJU Ocean College two months after he left. With her arrival, the new couple lived and studied together on the campus.

Shortly afterwards, Farhan's wife became pregnant. They were more than happy at the beginning of her pregnancy until, they were told in a routine inspection that the baby was not breathing and may not be healthy. More seriously, Farhan's wife was in danger of vein thrombus and cruor, a rare disease with unknown causes. If the thrombus got close to the important organs such as the heart, lungs, and brain, it could be life-threatening. Concurrent thrombosis during pregnancy made the problem even more complicated, as anticoagulant drugs may cause massive blood loss. The couple realized the genetic reason for the disease and knew how serious it could be, as several relatives from her family died from it.

Now it was her turn. Should they return to Pakistan or get treatment in China? They were faced with a tough moment to make a decision. At last, they chose to entrust it to the Chinese hospitals and doctors and sent her to the First Affiliated Hospital of Zhejiang University.

Farhan's wife had to have an abortion there and had to stay in hospital for a long time. It turned out that their decision was a wise one. She recovered soon after the effective treatment. When in retrospect, it was an extremely difficult time, as they passed through every suffering of anxiety, sorrow, and uncertainty. For Farhan, it was unforgettable to go through such a difficult time in China. It was even more unforgettable to witness the swiftness and the efficiency of the Chinese hospitals and doctors in the rescuing—from the receptionist to the in-patient ward, to the diagnosis, and to the treatment, not a minute was delayed in the whole process. During her stay, the nurses and the doctors were so kind and so helpful that she was recovered much sooner than expected. The couple was also grateful for the financial supports they got from the school, from the hospital, from their Chinese friends and some international friends whom they got to know at the school. They were able to be back to their routines in the university again.

Besides his wife's companionship, Farhan made many Chinese friends as well. In his spare time, he would take every opportunity participating in all kinds of campus events, learning and experiencing the Chinese culture. He learnt to play badminton and became a fan of this sport. He and his friend championed the men's double in a badminton game held by the Ocean College. From a beginner not knowing how to grab the racket to a champion, Farhan was greatly encouraged and kept challenging himself. At the New Year's party, he sang a song and was delighted by the audience's responses.

By hanging out with the Chinese teachers and friends, Farhan got to know more about the Chinese people. He saw the conscientiousness, sincerity, and kindness from them. If "everyone in this world has a different life and therefore a different way of thinking," then the Chinese are hospitable and kind, according to Farhan.

From January to February 2017, all the international students at the Ocean College went to Yuquan Campus for the president's Spring Festival party. Farhan was so interested in the event that he began to learn about the Chinese festivals and the customs on each festive day. In one of his classes, students were signed to make a presentation about China, Farhan chose to make an investigation about the red envelopes, as the Pakistanians use the so-called "Eidi" on Eid Adha, similar to the red envelopes on the Spring Festival.

Having lived in China for nearly two years, Farhan has not only learnt the professional knowledge but also acquired the culture. Besides Hangzhou, Farhan had been to Putuo island, which was called as "the Pearl of the East China Sea". He hoped to visit Beijing, Shanghai and other main cities in China, since it was a part of his study-abroad scheme.

Farhan's love for China was instilled by the friendship between the two countries. His love for the Chinese culture was like a microcosm of the China-Pakistan relationship. "The experience of studying in China will become a spiritual treasure throughout our lives," said the young couple.

With faith, I stand up to challenges

The research topic of Farhan and his supervisor was to study the gold mineralization in the northern Pakistan and China-Pakistan border regions, and to analyze the possibility of forming large and super gold deposits there.

Great minds think alike. Farhan and his instructor, Professor Ye Ying, chose the same topic. Before entering the school, Farhan had been engaged in the field geology and prospecting for several years. His initial research proposal was focused on the sand gold deposit on the northern plateau of Pakistan. After discussing with his instructor, Farhan shifted his research theme to the source of sand gold, in another word, the endogenous rock gold deposit.

Professor Ye asked Farhan a metaphoric question. If the local sand gold mines are like the stars, then the rock gold mine is like the moon. Pakistan has enough stars, but where is the moon? This metaphor was very vivid and appropriate for the situation in the northern mountainous area of Parkistan, where there are small-scaled sand gold mines in almost every stream and river channel, sufficient for the local people to buy their food and clothing by panning for gold in the streams, but not enough for industrialized mining, not to mention to support the social and economic development. On the other hand, in areas adjacent to Pakistan's northern plateau, from Kyrgyzstan to Afghanistan to China's Tibet in the western area, and to Myanmar in the eastern area, there are many large copper and gold deposits. These deposits are located in the same geographic area as the Pakistan's northern plateau, meaning they should have similar metallogenic conditions. Obviously, seeking for the moon was better than wasting time on the stars. Farhan accepted his professor's suggestions.

Professor Ye often said to his students: "Our research should not only be theoretically achieving, but also socially and economically influential." According to his students, Professor Ye is good at setting research goals for them in a skillful and visual way. They might be in the air for now, but as long as you work hard enough, you will finally end up getting there. This was also encouraging for Farhan. He never thought that Professor Ye depicted a dream out of reach. After all, will the Kashmir plateau be the brightest star in the starry sky? As the traffic artery path of the China-Pakistan Economic Corridor, there will be a highway and a railway linking Kashgar in Xinjiang and Gwadar in Pakistan. Besides, the large-scale hydropower plants and thermal power plants are also under construction. If geologists can make progresses in the geological exploration and mineralization of the gold deposits, the resources will be rapidly transformed into economic and social benefits. That way, both the countries and the

peoples will be soon benefited.

Naturally, it is not easy to achieve such a goal. It has to be noted that not only the local Pakistani companies, but also many foreign mineral companies have invested in the geological exploration in Kashmir. Many are well-equipped and experienced. However, the natural condition here is very different from that on the plain. If it were not for the valleys and streams, it is a sheer crude environment in which people have to go everywhere walking and communicate by shouting.

Before the summer vacation of 2017, Professor Ye and Farhan worked out a field work plan together. Potential mineralization was clearly in the mountains, and some were even close to the snow line. "My poor legs can't afford it to work in the field. It's on you." Professor Ye patted Farhan on the shoulder and said to him. He had never been to Pakistan, but he had been to the other side of the Kunlun Mountains some ten years ago, namely, the Pamirs in Xinjiang Autonomous Region, the plateau as huge and as tall as Kashmir. Professor Ye, no longer young, was like a hero being silent about his past glories. The young Farhan went further, with his enthusiasm for the exploration and with his professor's expectations for his growth.

Three months later, in mid-October, Farhan brought back about a hundred kilograms of sample stones from Kashmir.

Professor Ye might have questioned whether Farhan went into the mountains by riding a donkey or by driving a donkey cart, but he did not. All the hardship was shown on Farhan's badly tanned face, dark with some pink raw skin and reddish cheek, the clear mark of the past few months of living in the wild. The gleam in his eyes seemed to tell Professor Ye that he had brought back the hope of his people. The following work was also tough. For the far-away target set by Professor Ye, and for his and his nation's future, Farhan worked his best.

In the Ocean College, ZJU, the responsible and dedicated Professor Ye and his beloved student Farhan guarded a dream, the dream of Farhan, which was to receive better education, to obtain a doctorate degree, and to contribute to the development of mineral resources and the growth of economy in his hometown.

This is the dream of Farhan, a young geologist, for a great country and an affluent one. Keeping his initiative in mind, he would keep on pursuing his dream in China, regardless of the challenges ahead. Both Farhan and Professor Ye believe that someday Farhan's dream, started from ZJU, will be realized. The Moon will illuminate the Kashmir plateau, the economy there will boom, and Parkistan will develop quickly. The people will dance to the tambourine and guitar in the "moonlight" to celebrate their better life.

是学，更是爱

一个人的学习生涯，能够记录多远的距离？

是在使命的召唤下，从喀麦隆到相距万里的中国，从地上到海下的研究。

一位来华留学生，在短短一年中，对中国会有着怎样的感情？

他学会校歌，迷上太极，将导师视为在中国的家人，对这片土地和在其上的人怀着纯粹的爱。

2017年，来自喀麦隆的高明被自己国家的政府选中获得来华深造的机会，并在中国政府奖学金的支持下，在这个最好的时代里开始了他全新的学习生涯与人生经历。一段中国缘也自此开始。

收到浙江大学录取通知书时的那份喜悦感，以及对喀麦隆和中国政府的感激之情是无法用言语来描述的。能到有"东方剑桥"美誉的浙江大学来深造，对高明来说，意味着将拥有更为辽阔的发展空间、更为丰富的学习机会、更高层次的发展目标。他甚至不知道该去感谢谁，但他切实为自己的幸运而感到激动，也将这份感激埋在心里，化为前行的动力。

没有丝毫的犹豫，高明告离故土，别了家人，义无反顾地踏上了中国大地，来到浙江大学。

高明的家人纷纷支持他到浙江大学深造的决定，尤其是他的妻子。其实此时距高明成婚仅仅一个月，本是该享受蜜月的新婚燕尔却要面临分离。看着即将远赴他乡求学的丈夫，妻子心中免不了离别的伤感，但心想丈夫此行是要

高明与其新婚妻子
Gao Ming and his newly-wedded wife

获得更高层次的教育，是为了整个家庭，同时也担负着祖国的使命，她感到开心与值得。面对丈夫要留学中国的决定，她和家人一致地支持。正是身后的这份有力支持，让高明能安心在中国学习，并能保持不断进步的动力。

　　初到中国，高明心中有着身处异国的陌生与寂寥。在这个全新的国度里，周围都是从未谋面的师生，加之学习内容上的大不同，让高明感到一丝慌张。对于大多数的留学生来说，这也是正常的，他们往往要经历一个较为漫长的适应期才能安顿下来，在这之前，很难完全沉心于自己应做的事业。然而，高明自己也没料到，他的这份陌生感很快消失在周围师生的和谐氛围之中。"友善"是中国人留给高明最深的印象，他常说："上帝在造人的时候，赋予了中国人更多的谦卑品质。"从步履未稳的孩童，到充满朝气的青年，直至最美夕阳的老年人，高明发现他们总是面带微笑，相互之间充满尊敬，对待非洲同学格外关照，这份融洽的感觉使他仿佛身处家中。

高明在公园里与中国小朋友一起
Gao Ming with some Chinese children
in the park

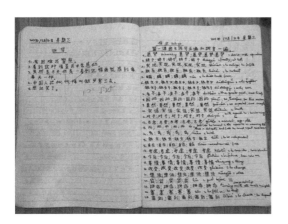

高明的中文作业
Gao Ming's Chinese class assignments

刚入学时，高明曾在骑自行车途中意外摔倒，身边的中国同学立即送他就医。好在并无大碍，但这份来自周围素不相识的中国同学的热心与善良，让高明着实为之感动。

即使是在专注深奥的课堂学习中，老师也总是微笑鼓励，带动学生的思维。学生一心一意，与老师保持交流，整个课堂氛围轻松却收获颇丰。在高明眼中，讲台上的老师是真正沉浸于教育事业与课堂之中的。他认为，这是一股源于国家的力量，老师和同学都是朋友般的存在，每个人都是值得去学习的榜样。"三人行，必有我师"，这句话在高明身上得到了最好的体现。老师的循循善诱，让高明感到自己也变得更为聪明，在这样轻松专注的课堂氛围中，他上课学习的积极性得到了大幅度的提高。

在喀麦隆时，高明曾担任渔业工程师，也曾任职海军机械师，现在主要从事海洋鱼类行为的研究。相比以往，现在所学知识和之前的工作经历有着较大差异。海洋学院为他配备了强大的导师团队：叶瑛教授，主要研究方向是海洋地质；邵庆均教授，主要研究方向是水产动物；海外归来的年轻博士黄慧老师，主要研究方向是海洋工程技术。几位导师共同努力，助力高明的进步成才。

经过几番讨论，结合高明自身的意

高明参加2017年APEC研讨会
Gao Ming in the 2017 APEC seminar

愿特点，导师们为他制订了专门的培养计划，前期学习水下观测、信息处理技术，为后期的鱼类行为研究奠定基础。观察分析鱼类行为需要大量的样本监测，探索影响因子需要不断的实验，还要实现在水下的观测与信息处理利用，这注定是一个复杂的学习过程，却有着极重大的现实意义。高明已经计划在本学年的夏学期，为研究工作作开题报告。同时他也不断查阅相关文献，制订初步的博士论文研究计划，几位导师帮助高明再细化、深化研究计划，确保在暑期前他可以正式开展研究工作。

喀麦隆地处沿海，高明所学对自己的国家建设也有着极大的意义。高明被安排在一个团队中学习，这不仅仅是为了他专业上的突破，更为重要的是学习的过程，是在此期间锻炼提升分析问题、解决问题的能力与思路方法。这正是浙江大学的育人理念所在，即让每位学生都获得"知识、能力、素质、人格"的全面发展，培养具有国际视野的未来领导者和创新型人才。

叶瑛老师对待自己的学生从来都是亦师亦友，关心照料着学生学习科研、生活起居的点点滴滴。高明眼中的叶老师，也更像是一位家人，彼此携手共进才共同构成了留学生项目。叶老师常常与高明分析在本阶段该学什么、如何去学，帮助他慢慢适应这个学习的过程。邵庆均老师时常教导高明，年轻人应当有海纳百川的包容胸怀，多感知和适应中国文化对他的进步有着非同小可的促进作用。

中国对高明来说，似乎有着天然的吸引力。初入校门，他就被《浙江大学校歌》的优雅旋律所吸引，一首"大不自多，海纳江河"蕴含着浙江大学的辽阔胸怀，让高明为之感动。学校四处可见的校歌标示更坚定了他要学会这首歌的决心。都知道《浙江大学校歌》意境深远却晦涩难懂，即便是土生土长的中国学生也要费上一番工夫才能领会其含义。高明对于校歌的喜爱，远大于要为之付出的辛苦，他将歌词的汉字和拼音一笔一笔写下来，在网上找到校歌的音频并跟随练习。通过苦练自学，他做到了能和中国学生一样唱好校歌，为之的付出是可想而知了。

高明也喜欢太极拳，对于其中的基本招式更是熟记于心。太极拳是中国的传统武术，在一招一式、动静虚实间传达着中国人所信奉的人生哲学。高明把太极认作一种"美"。确实，太极源于自然，天地有大美而不言。能感受到太

高明练习太极拳
Gao Ming practicing Tai Chi

极中蕴含的美，是高明对中国文化的深刻体验。

邵老师说，他很开心看到高明能很好地融入中国文化，这对高明无论是适应生活，还是以后更好地发展都有着极大的帮助。

在高明到浙江大学一段时间后，他在家乡的妻子顺利产下女儿，这是他们的第一个孩子。初为人父的高明急切地想要尽到一名父亲的责任，想把女儿轻轻抱在怀里、教给她为人处世的道理、给她讲美妙的童话故事……但两地相隔甚远，家人之间只能在网络下透过屏幕进行交流，传递互相的思念。即便是这样，高明也感到满足，新生的女儿让他有了更为充沛的行动力。学校为此特意邀请了高明的家人到中国来生活一段时间，这让他既意外又惊喜。在和最重要的人在一起的时间里，高明的生活更加幸福美满，内心愈加平静，在学业成绩上也取得了飞快的进步。

十年树木，百年树人，教育是一个民族发展的灵魂所在。高明有感于祖国的教育事业尚不完善，渴盼回到家乡后做一名教师，传道授业，育人子弟。他希望能将自己成长中所积累的点点滴滴，尤其是在中国、在浙大所学到的知识，传授给更多的家乡人，推动家乡教育的发展。今日，高明在浙江大学叶老师、邵老师门下接受春风雨露，将来归国也必然会是桃李芬芳，为家乡的教育带来新风尚。

　　或许在高明心里，他已经把中国、把浙江大学当成了他的第二个"故乡"。在这里，有亲如家人的导师，有值得见贤思齐的同学，有热情友善的人们，又有谁不会爱上这里？一年里的收获，让他深深爱上这片土地。虽然是"被选择"到的中国，但高明发自内心感激当初这个机会给了自己。

　　高明在浙江大学，是学，更是爱。

高明与朋友们一起
Gao Ming with friends

采访人：张鸿乾

采访日期：2018年3月

I Learn, I Love

How far can a person's journey of learning be recorded?

With a mission, it is from Cameroon to China, from the ground to the bottom of the sea.

How does an international student feel about China after living here for a year?

He learned the School Anthem, marveled at Tai Chi boxing, and took his instructor as his family in China, all full of passion for this land and its people.

In 2017, Gao Ming, came from Cameroon, was granted by the government the opportunity of studying in China. With the support of the Chinese government scholarship, he began his new life in this best era. His destiny with China began ever since.

He could barely find a word to describe his joy upon receiving the admission from Zhejiang University and his gratitude for the Cameroon and the Chinese governments. This opportunity to the university, known as the "Oriental Cambridge", means a broader horizon for his development, a more colorful learning experience, and a higher goal to achieve. He did not even know whom to thank, but he was really excited for the luck. Keeping that thankfulness deep in his heart, he was more motivated to march forward.

Without hesitation, Gao Ming left his homeland, said goodbye to his family, came to China and to Zhejiang University.

Gao Ming's family gave him full support, especially his wife, who had just married him for one month. Their honeymoon had turned into a departure. Seeing her husband off, the bride was melancholy. But thinking that her husband's trip to get further education was for the good of the whole family and for the mission of the country, she found it worthwhile. It was this strong support from her and the family that allows Gao Ming feel at ease in China and with a continuous momentum.

Upon his arrival, Gao Ming was overwhelmed by loneliness in a foreign country. Surrounded by the first-met teachers and students, plus the differences in the learning once made Gao Ming a bit panic. For most of the international students, this is a normal reaction— they usually have to go through a relatively long time to settle down. They could barely concentrate on their study until then. However, it was out of Gao Ming's expectation that his feeling of strange was gone really soon in the harmonious atmosphere among the teachers and the students. "Nice and friendly" is what he would say about the Chinese, "It seems that when

God created them, he puts a great amount of his humility potion in them," said Gao Ming. From peddlers to the vigorous young, and to the aged, Gao Ming finds that they always wear the smiling faces and respect each other. They treat the African students with special care. The feeling of harmony makes him feel like in a big family.

When he first arrived at the school, Gao Ming had an accident while riding his bike. The passers-by helped him to the hospital as soon as possible. He was lucky that he wasn't hurt in the accident. The affection and attention of the strangers moved him greatly.

Even in the esoteric course learning, the teachers always smile and encourage the students to think, while the students are concentrated and communicative, and the classes relaxing but rewarding. To Gao Ming, the teachers are really devoted to education. He believes that this is a vigor that originates from the country—teachers and students being friends like and everyone is worthy of learning from. As Confucius said, "When some three men are together, each of them can always be learned from." This was best seen in Gao Ming, who found himself more intelligently inspired by the teachers. In such relaxing yet intensive classes, he became more enthusiastic for participating.

While in Cameroon, Gao Ming was a fishery engineer and used to be a technician in the Navy, studying marine fish behavior. Compared to the past, what he is learning now is very different. Nevertheless, the Ocean College has provided him with a strong team of instructors: Prof. Ye Ying, an expert at marine geology; Prof. Shao Qingjun, studying aquatic animals; Prof. Huang Hui, a young doctor returned from overseas and focused on marine engineering technology. They worked together to help Gao Ming in his study.

Considering Gao Ming's conditions and his wishes, the professors worked out a specific curriculum for him after several discussions—learning underwater observation and information processing techniques in the early stage to get prepared for the later study into fish behavior. Observing and analyzing fish behavior means monitoring a large quantity of samples, whereas constant experimentation, underwater observation, and information processing and utilization are heeded in the seek for the influence factors. This is bound to be a complicated yet extremely practical learning process. Gao Ming is to make his theses proposal in the summer. Meanwhile, he's reading a whole lot of references and documents to make a preliminary research plan for his doctoral dissertation. The professors helped him deepen and refine it to ensure that he could formally carry out research work before the summer vacation.

Cameroon is a coastal country. What he has learned is also of great significance to the construction of his country. Gao Ming was arranged to study in a team, not only for his professional breakthroughs, but more importantly the process of learning and the growth of the abilities and the way of thinking when analyse and solve problems. This is the concept of Zhejiang University in terms of education—to make the students develop all over in knowledge, ability, quality, and personality, and to make them into the future leaders and the innovative talents with international visions.

Prof. Ye has always been a teacher and a friend to his students, caring for their learning, research, and lives. For Gao Ming, Prof. Ye is a teacher but also a family member going through his study abroad program hand-in-hand with him. Prof. Ye often discusses with Gao Ming what to learn and how to learn, and helps him to gradually adapt to the learning program. Prof. Shao makes Gao Ming understand that young people should be open-minded. The in-depth perception of the Chinese culture has a positive effect in his progresses.

For Gao Ming, China seems to have a natural attraction. When first got to the school, he was attracted by the beautiful university anthem—"The vast sea contains all streams, all rivers." This broad-mindedness and absorbing spirit of Zhejiang University sung in the anthem made Gao Ming so touched that he made up his mind to learn the song. It is posted almost everywhere in the school and is known for its profoundness and difficulty. Even the Chinese students have to take a while to understand its meaning. Gao Ming's love for the school anthem outweighs the hard work he has to do. He wrote down the Chinese characters and pinyin word for word, learning after the recording he found on the Internet. By practicing and persistence, he can sing the song as well as his Chinese peers.

Gao Ming also likes Tai Chi boxing. He remembers all the moves and gestures. Tai Chi is a traditional Chinese martial art. It conveys the Chinese philosophy of life in every of its move and action, defense and attack. Gaoming thinks Tai Chi is beautiful. Indeed, Tai Chi originates from the nature, which nurtures everything without a word. Being able to understand the beauty in Tai Chi is his finest understanding of the Chinese culture.

Professor Shao is very pleased to see that Gao Ming has adjusted himself very well to the Chinese culture. He believes that this is of great help to Gao Ming, whether it is to adapt to a new life, or to have a better future.

Months after Gao Ming came to Zhejiang University, his wife gave birth to their first child, a girl. He was so anxious to hold her in his arms, teaching her the truth of life, and telling her the wonderful stories... But they are so far apart that they can only communicate via video phones. Even so, Gao Ming is contented and initiated by his new-born daughter. The school administrators gave special invitation to Gao Ming's family for them to live in China

with him for some time. This was an unexpected surprise to him. In the time living with his beloved, Gao Ming was excited, but kept calm with his study, making rapid progresses.

Ten years are needed to plant a tree, while a hundred years to bring up a nation. Education is the soul of a nation's development. Gao Ming, realizing that the education in his country is yet to be developed, he is eager to become a teacher after returning home, teaching children. He hopes that with his accumulated knowledge, especially with what he has learnt in China and at Zhejiang University, he will be able to teach more people in his hometown and promote the development of the country's education. Today, what Gao Ming is learning after Prof. Ye and Prof. Shao at Zhejiang University will hopefully bring something new to the education back at his home after he goes back.

Perhaps Gao Ming compared China and Zhejiang University to his second hometown, where he met quite a few family-like professors, outstanding classmates, and friendly people. Who could not love this place? The gains in the year left him a profound love for this piece of land. Although he was not the one who chose to come to China, Gao Ming was sincerely grateful for being chosen to come.

Gao Ming's stay in Zhejiang University was to learn and was more to love.

心中装着一片海

迎风而起

从故乡巴基斯坦来华留学前，努尔已经和海洋研究相伴了十余年。自2000年起，努尔在巴基斯坦国家海洋研究所的物理海洋学研究团队工作，并作为团队的研究骨干从事着物理海洋方面的研究。多次的实地考察经验让他对收集环境、气象和潮汐、波浪等相关的海洋水文资料、部署海洋仪器等现场工作十分熟悉。

早已迈入工作岗位并经验颇丰的努尔，因何选择来到中国留学呢？此中有着不少契机。驱使他从巴基斯坦来中国的三个主要理由是，浙江大学同巴基斯坦国家海洋研究所的合作关系、他对冒险活动的热爱以及在他的国家不具备的进一步的研究能力。

首先，努尔所在的巴基斯坦国家海洋研究所是巴基斯坦最重要的海洋研究机构，这个机构与浙江大学海洋学院、自然资源部第二海洋研究所有着良好的长期合作关系，在科研人员培训、研究生培养、科研合作交流等方面开展了紧密合作。2013年春，在中巴国际合作项目的资助下，努尔与他的三名同事一起，在中国自然资源部第二海洋研究所开展了为期5个月的合作研究。在此基础上，2013年夏，努尔申请获得了中国政府海洋奖学金资助，得到了博士研究生留学资格。

再者，努尔有着排除万难的强烈留学意愿。要知道，努尔早已有了妻子，也是多个孩子的父亲，作为一家之主，他承担着支撑家庭的责任。在这样的情况下，离开家乡绝非易事，毕竟，他已经不再是"无牵无挂"的少年，他有着对亲人深深的眷恋与牵挂。纵然如此，努尔同样知道，这眷恋与牵挂应当转化为前进的动力。中国有着优良的科研环境和先进的设备与技术，作为巴基斯坦海洋研究领域重要的科研人员，他的科研目标需要借助中国的教育得以圆满地实现。他表示，在离开家乡、离开祖国前，他已做好了充分的心理准备。家庭固然重要，而为祖国做出自己的贡献亦是努尔生命的重要内容。通情达理的妻子深谙丈夫的志向和抱负，全力支持他来中国留学。

浙江大学海洋学院让他的这份"坚决"得到了应有的价值。在导师贺治国教授的带领下，努尔着手研究起了自己最感兴趣也急于研究探索的印度河河口海洋动力过程研究项目。具体来讲，努尔的研究工作是首次系统地对巴基斯坦最大的河口进行现场观测并构建了三维数值模型开展详细的研究分析。该河口处于印度洋阿拉伯海沿岸，濒临巴基斯坦最大的港口城市卡拉奇。努尔发现巴基斯坦沿海常受海洋的侵害，频发的盐水入侵、河口侵蚀等灾害对沿岸地区的渔业发展、工程建设等非常不利。努尔认为，为了治理海洋沿岸及河口地区的生态环境，让巴基斯坦的人们能在那块区域安居乐业、发展经济，必须对该河口的径流和海洋动力过程进行全面而深入的了解，这样才能有效解决遇到的实际问题。这个研究工作的成果将对该港口的城市建设、航道和岸线的综合治

努尔在巴基斯坦沿海采样
Noor sampling at the coast of Pakistan

努尔独自在实验室学习
Noor studying alone in the lab

努尔与导师贺治国教授一起
Noor with his instructor Prof. He Zhiguo

理、近海生态修复等具有重要的意义。同时，作为中国的友好邻邦，这项研究也将对巴基斯坦与中国合作开展"海上丝绸之路"的建设起到重要的科学支撑作用。

这项研究，可谓任重道远。在浙江大学海洋学院求学的三年多里，努尔参与了课题组的研究工作并多次参加学术活动。在第四届JCOMM亚太区域海洋仪器检测技术研讨会上，努尔还积极地作了发言，进行了主题报告，详细介绍了巴基斯坦在海岸研究方面所作出的努力及成果。为了获得更多、更真实的数据，2015年，在巴基斯坦国家海洋局相关基金的资助下，努尔参与了在印度河三角洲的胡拜尔海湾的野外调查，获得了胡拜尔海湾雨季期间完整涨落潮周期内的水温、浊度、盐度、潮位和潮流等第一手观测数据。通过在一个漫长雨季里耐心细致的观测调查，努尔对此海域内的径流和潮流动力特性进行了有效的研究，收获颇多。努尔对近海的实践调查已非常习惯，无论是船只颠簸还是骄阳似火，努尔都已当成家常便饭。面对着广阔的天空和洋面，看到那带点神秘的蓝色交会的地平线，努尔感受到了大自然的力量，也在夕阳西下的静谧景色中体会到了无法用语言描述的震撼。他知道，正是这壮阔美丽的海洋，给人们以希望，但有时也给人们带来灾难。他希望人们总能看到家乡的美丽，而不要在海水的肆虐中哭泣。

在舟山校区学习时，努尔将大部分时间花在了学业上，他长时间待在图书馆、实验室内。回想起校园生活，他认为自己是个专注学习的学生，而且非常感谢贺治国教授给予他的支持。

贺治国教授对努尔的工作给予充分理解，他在努尔所研究的领域有较深造诣，时常给出有益的建议，和努尔探讨研究工作的进度，对努尔的研究最终取得成功起到了至关重要的作用。努尔毕业时已在高水平国际SCI期刊上发表了3篇学术论文。除了学习，贺治国教授也十分关心努尔的生活并给予了他最大的尊重和支持。知道努尔有个很大的家庭，在放假前贺治国教授总会贴心地给努尔的孩子们准备一些小礼物，带去他真诚的问候。在平时的学习生活中，导师贺治国与努尔的交谈总是温和愉快的，导师贺治国将努尔当作朋友来对待，而努尔也对导师有着深深的感情，对他的帮助和关心怀着感激之情。

努尔在课题组组会上发言
Noor giving a presentation in the meeting of his research group

努尔的博士论文答辩
Noor defending his doctoral thesis

随潮而来

如今，在浙江大学海洋学院留学过的努尔已经对中国有些熟悉并怀着眷恋了。在中国，他留下了太多美好的回忆。

还记得刚来到浙大的两个月，努尔适应中国环境遇到的第一个障碍就是吃不惯中国菜，但经过一段时间积极的尝试和适应，努尔慢慢变成了一个"中餐迷"。他很喜欢中餐烹饪蔬菜的方法，并乐于品尝各个地区的美食。他去过的中国城市有不少：北京、天津、威海、成都、上海等。每个城市都给他留下了深刻的印象，比如北京带着首都风范的建筑，天津熙熙攘攘的闹市，成都独特的地理环境与色香味极佳的川菜，威海的沿海风情等。他感受到中国之大，各地都有各地的风貌特色，各地都有着美好的人文底蕴，而这些风景和文化与他的故乡巴基斯坦有着很大的差别。

努尔也忘不了他的中国朋友们以及与他们度过的时光。努尔的中国朋友们会带他去中国餐厅吃饭，大家一起聊天吃菜，好不欢乐。在船上进行调查任务时，努尔也与中国朋友们互相合作，在休闲时进行轻松的交流。会使用中国的社交软件后，努尔在社交平台上也秀出了他与中国朋友们的合影，照片上大家满脸笑意。从中国朋友身上，他也能看到中国的文化。在努尔的眼里，不论是中国的老师、同学，还是素不相识的陌生人，都对他非常友好，他觉得中国朋友非常"有观察力"，能及时并细致地给予他关心与帮助。在中国，努尔认真地学习了中文，在日常对话中，努尔能说些"谢谢""不好意思"等常用语，大方地和中国人交流。

当思念远方家人的时候，努尔会借助微信的视频通话功能与妻儿交流，因为彼此心意相通，中巴之间的几万里也就不那么遥远了。

努尔参加浙江大学学位授予仪式
Noor in the degree conferment ceremony of ZJU

从浙起航

　　踏实稳重的努尔是浙江大学海洋学院第一个博士毕业的留学生。他迎风而起，随潮而来。现在看来，努尔是一个心怀理想的开拓者，是一个专心学业的研究者，他的浙大求学经历必将帮助他未来在巴基斯坦海洋研究领域取得成就。在努尔的心中一直装着一片海，那片海在家乡，也在"浙里"。在巴基斯坦国家海洋局时，努尔关注的印度河河口生态和环境问题，被他牢牢抓住不放，带着建设家国、服务人民的梦想，努尔在浙江大学努力学习，攻读博士学位。学成之后，他以拳拳之心，将把在中国这个友好邻邦学到的知识带回祖国巴基斯坦，继续研究工作。有了数据基础和知识储备，努尔学成回国后付诸实践，研究工作进展得非常顺利。体会到中国的教育优势，努尔也希望更多的巴基斯坦的学生们来中国留学，接受良好的高等教育。

　　三年半的"浙里"时光不知不觉流逝了，留学生努尔穿上了浙江大学的毕业服，在熟悉的校园里拍下了毕业照。拿到毕业证书的那天，努尔心里想的是什么呢？是舟山安静和谐的校园，是导师的话语和在实验室的日夜，抑或是巴基斯坦港口的阵阵涛声，梦寐以盼的轮船为家乡载去安宁？

采访人：张明珉

采访日期：2018年3月

努尔与一起毕业的研究生在竺可桢像前合影
Noor with other graduate students in front of the statue of Chu Kochen

I Love the Ocean

Rise with the wind

Before coming to China, Noor had been doing oceanographic research for more than ten years in Pakistan. Since 2000 He joined the physical oceanographic research team at the Pakistan National Institute of Oceanography (NIO), working on physical oceanography. During his field work, he became familiar with collecting information on environment, meteorology, tide, and wave, with placing ocean study instruments, and with every other relevant topic within the oceanography field.

Despite his previous experiences and high level of success, he chose to relocate to China. The three major reasons that motivated him to move to China is the partnership between Zhejiang University with NIO in Pakistan, his love for adventure, and the additional research potential that was not present in his country.

First, as the most important marine research institute in the country, NIO has long-term cooperation with the Zhejiang University's Ocean College and with the Second Institute of Oceanography under Ministry of Natural Resources of China. The cooperation between China and Pakistan focuses on the areas of training researchers, running graduate programs, and doing scientific researches. In the spring of 2013, Noor, sponsored by the China-Pakistan international cooperation project, along with three of his colleagues, embarked on a five-month joint study at the SIO in China. In the summer of the year, Noor was awarded the marine scholarship from the Chinese government, and was enrolled as a doctorate candidate in oceanography.

Noor's desire to study abroad was so strong that nothing could stop him. As a husband and a father, he was the only bread earner of his family. It was obviously difficult for him to get away from home. Despite of his love and care for his family, Noor was determined to come to China. The well-funded scientific research environment and the advanced equipment in China benefited his research. As Noor said, he was well-prepared for contributing to his country even before leaving his home. His wife, knowing his ambition, gave him her full supports.

The offer of the Zhejiang University's Ocean College deserved all his resolution and efforts. Noor did researches under the instructions of Prof. He Zhiguo, getting into the ocean dynamic process of the Indus river estuary. The topic interests him and was urgently in need of study. More specifically, Noor's research was the first systematic field study into the largest estuary in Pakistan and the first detailed research using an analysis via a three-dimensional numerical model. The estuary is on the Arabian Sea coast in the Indian Ocean and is close to Karachi, Pakistan's largest port city. Noor is very concerned about the frequent saltwater flooding and estuarine erosion because it is detrimental to the commercial growth in the region. Noor believes that a comprehensive and in-depth understanding of the estuary's runoff with the ocean dynamic processes is necessary. Noor wants to make an ecological and habitable coastal area with healthy estuary area for the Pakistani people to thrive. The results of his research will be of great significance to the construction of the port cities, the comprehensive waterways and the coast line management, and to the ecology restoration in the offshore areas. At the same time, as a friendly neighbor of China, this study will also play an important role in Pakistan and China's joint construction of the Maritime Silk Road.

Started three years ago, this research was in its infancy. While studying in the Zhejiang University Ocean College, Noor participated in the research as a group member and attended some academic events. In the fourth JCOMM Asia-Pacific regional symposium on the marine instrument detection technology, Noor gave a speech on the goals and the achievements of the Pakistan's coastal research. In 2015, the Pakistan State Ocean Administration created a field investigation into the Indus river delta Khobar creek bay, as an effort to get more real time data. As a member of the field investigation team, Noor collected the first-hand data of its water temperature, turbidity, salinity, tide, and current in a complete tide cycle in the rainy season. Being primarily in the Khobar creek bay during the rainy season to gain research data on the runoff and tidal dynamics in the bay, he became so accustomed to the off-coast field studies that he took the rocking boat and the scorching sun as normal. The research environment reaffirmed his passion for the miracle of the ocean and the beauty of the nature, especially the tranquility in the setting sun. He realized that this splendid and beautiful ocean could bring people opportunity. He hopes that all people could see the beauty of the natural environment along the coast and feel blessed even though the ocean is a devastating force along with its ability to give life to our civilization.

While studying at Zhejiang University Zhoushan campus, Noor spent most of his time studying, hanging out in the libraries and the oceanography labs. As he recalled his campus life, he was always reminded that a great professor should assist learning. In this sense, he owes a debt of gratitude towards Professor He Zhiguo.

Professor He was well aware of Noor's work and was an expert in Noor's research field. He gave Noor advices, discussed with Noor his progress in the research, and played a vital role in Noor's achievements. Upon graduation, Noor published three SCI papers in several prestigious international academic journals. In addition to his studies, Professor He also supported Noor in his daily life. Knowing that Noor had a large family, Prof. He would prepare some gifts before holidays for Noor's children and send them his best wishes. Prof. He treated Noor like a friend, and in turn, he treated his instructor with gratitude.

Come with the tide

After studying in the Zhejiang University Ocean College, Noor is not only familiar with China but is a little sentimental for it. China has a central part in Noor's success.

In his first two months at Zhejiang University, Noor's first challenge to adapt himself to the environment in China was the local food. After a while of active trying and adapting, he gradually becomes a Chinese food lover. He likes Chinese way of cooking vegetables, and is willing to try different food from different regions. He has visited many Chinese cities: Beijing, Tianjin, Weihai, Chengdu, Shanghai, and so on. Noor has a specific impression on each city—the classical capital Beijing, the hustling and bustling Tianjin, the unique landscape and excellent food in Chengdu, and the coastal breeze in Weihai. The size and historical achievements of China captivate Noor and encourage him to explore his adopted land. Noor is proud to be from Pakistan but is invigorated to learn everything he can about his adopted home that has nurtured his ambition. He is well aware that there are fine differences between Pakistan and China. He is also well aware that there are big differences from person to person, but the joy of life lies in finding the unique qualities that everyone has.

Noor could never forget his Chinese friends nor the time he spent with them. They would take him to a Chinese restaurant for dinner, chatting while eating. The field study ship allowed Noor to create a bond with his Chinese research fellows that will stay with him personally and professionally. Noor is an active user of the Chinese social media, Noor published his pictures with his Chinese friends on his WeChat moments. According to Noor, whether it was his Chinese teacher or his classmates, or a complete stranger, they were all very friendly, considerate, and helpful. Noor studied Chinese during his stay and could say rudimentary words, such as "thank you" and "sorry", etc. to communicate with the Chinese people.

When he got homesick, he would call his family via WeChat. The internet has revolutionized every aspect of his life and has made the distance between places neglectable.

Set sail from Zhejiang University

Mature and steadfast, Noor was the first expat PhD graduated from the Zhejiang University Ocean College. Rising with the wind and coming with the tide, Noor is an explorer with great expectations in all aspects of his life. His experiences at Zhejiang University will help him further his marine research once he returns to Pakistan. Noor always has his ocean dream, at home and at Zhejiang University. When he was in the Pakistan State Ocean Administration, Noor focused on the Indus river estuary's ecological and environmental problems. With the dream of serving the people of Pakistan, he came to Zhejiang University and earned his doctorate degree. Upon completing his study, he went back to Pakistan with the knowledge he learned in China to continue his research. With the data base and the knowledge reserve, Noor is doing very well with his work in Pakistan. Being aware of the advantages of his education in China, Noor also hopes to convince more Pakistan students to come to China for higher education.

The three and half years in Zhejiang went by so fast that when Noor put on his Zhejiang University commencement gown for graduation photos on the familiar campus, he couldn't believe how much of himself had been left in Zhejiang. What was Noor thinking of on the day when he got his diploma? Was it the quiet and peaceful Zhoushan campus, or Professor He, or the days and nights in the lab, or the splashing waves at the Pakistani port, or the ship in his dreams that would carry the treasure and tranquility to his country?

他走过山海，终抵达高处

爱德华（右2）参加"大洋一号"航次科考
Edward (right 2nd) in the science expedition of Ocean One

2012年，在尼日利亚国家海洋研究所主任、大陆架界限委员会主席阿沃西卡的邀请下，执行大洋科考第26航次任务的中国"大洋一号"科考船在尼日利亚领海开展了为期半月的科学考察。来自尼日利亚国家海洋研究所的爱德华参与了这次科考，与中国科学家共同完成了本航次调查任务。这个航次填补了尼日利亚外海海洋地质、地球物理调查的空白，同时也架起了爱德华来中国的桥梁。

当时，对于杭州，甚至是中国，爱德华完全没有概念，仅有的一点了解来自与中国科学家的半个月合作的接触。但就是这半个月的合作，让他对中国这个东方大国产生了向往。一切像是冥冥之中的安排，这年恰逢中国政府设立海洋奖学金，爱德华格外珍惜这个机会，就选择了申请到中国留学深造。这份契机显得既意外却又合理，2013年9月2日，爱德华在浙江大学报到注册，正式成为浙江大学的一名留学生。

起步比想象中顺利，都说留学生要经历一段适应新环境的时间，爱德华却并没有对这块未曾踏足过的土地感到陌生，便捷的通信手段也缓解了他对家人的牵挂。在一切都安顿好后，爱德华开始了在浙江大学的课程学习，并到自然资源部第二海洋研究所（以下简称海洋二所）参与科学研究。他研究的对象就是中尼合作航次在大西洋采集的沉积物岩芯。他要利用大西洋沉积物岩芯研究大西洋热带区域的古气候与古环境的演变。他希望在中国的学习能使自己的科研水平得到进一步提高，计划在归国后继续为尼日利亚的海洋科学研究贡献力量。

爱德华的导师是资深海洋专家韩喜球教授。韩教授重视对学生的培养，每周定期召开组会讨论研究进展，由于每位团队成员的研究内容不尽相同，通过组会，爱德华从中学习到不少新知识，得到不少新启发。爱德华很喜欢课题组的组会制度和团队协作精神。

韩喜球教授对于学生的态度是关心而认真的，她治学严谨，对待学生的科研工作更是一丝不苟。对待爱德华将要投稿的论文，从词句到内容，韩教授都会亲自反复修改。她要求学生不仅要提高科研能力，科学写作素养也不容忽

爱德华（左3）与导师韩喜球教授（右2）一起参加中非海洋科技论坛
Edward(left 3rd) in the China–Africa Forum on Marine Science and
Technology with his supervisor Han Xiqiu (right 2nd)

视。"科研论文要反复打磨，我不允许质量不过关的论文拿出去投稿。"

在这几年的时间里，爱德华获得了很多机会，包括参加了一系列学术会议。2014年4月22日至23日，爱德华代表海洋二所在厦门参加了"第四届海洋科学与法律问题国际研讨会（Fourth

爱德华参加第六届全国沉积学大会
Edward in the 6th National Sedimentological Congress

International Symposium on Scientific and Legal Aspects of the Regimes of the Continental Shelf and the Area）"；2015年9月25日至27日参加了"第三届国际洋中脊理论研讨会"；2017年10月28日在南京大学召开的第六届全国沉积学大会（The 6th National Sedimentological Congress）上，他作了题为"来自东赤道大西洋深海盆地的深海浊度岩"（Deep sea turbidites from the abyssal basin of eastern Equatorial Atlantic）的口头报告。

爱德华(右3)博士学位论文答辩时与阿沃西卡教授(右2)和导师韩喜球教授(左3)合影
Edward's(right 3rd) PhD dissertation defense with Professor Awosika (right 2nd) and Professor Han Xiqiu (left 3rd)

爱德华的身体状况不太好，为此，他的导师韩喜球教授给他准备了血压监测计，他也总是随身携带。在尼日利亚时，爱德华的收入水平属于当地的中上等，但由于要供养两个孩子读书、承担赡养老人的责任，再除去日常花销，他往往也是只能达到收支相抵的状态。因为到浙大留学，中国政府为爱德华提供了每个月3500元人民币的生活费资助，学费、住宿费、医疗保险也都一一由学校为他解决，韩喜球教授每月再额外提供他1400元人民币的生活补助。这样，爱德华每月还能把结余寄回国补贴家用。

2014年，在国家海洋局与浙江大学的联合组织下，爱德华到首都北京参观了长城和故宫。在巍峨的长城上，他饱览了中国大地的壮丽河山。这次北京之行留下的美好回忆陪伴了爱德华很长一段时间。

爱德华之前不曾想到，尽管中国人口极众，但身边的一切都是那么井然有序。地铁四通八达，街区繁华整洁，平时的交通和外出旅行既便利又便宜。在与同学的接触中，每位同学都非常热情、友善。他也很热情开朗，在平时乘公交车往返宿舍与实验室的途中，会有些中国乘客主动与他聊天，并加他微信，他从来不拒绝。这样一来二去，他的生活中又多了许多的朋友。

科研中严肃以待，生活中师生情浓。在韩喜球教授的朋友圈里，有这样一张图片，内容是一个装着零食的塑料瓶，这是爱德华从家乡带来的小礼物。几年的在华留学时光，注定是终生难忘的，爱德华获得的不仅有知识的增长，还有科学素养的提高。挥一挥衣袖阔别中国，尽管不带走一片云彩，但那份情谊却早已镌刻在心头。

爱德华对于自己的未来很笃定，不回头，不低头，眼中有路，心中有光，为海洋事业尽心尽力。他是幸运的，遇到了好的契机、好的环境、好的导师；他是努力的，于是抵达了自己所期望的高处。对于现在的所得，他最多的情绪是感激，"感谢中国政府和我的导师，和团队里帮助我的人"。鹏之于飞，逆风千里；水涌孤舟，激浪开迎。

采访人：张鸿乾

采访日期：2018年4月

Crossing over Seas and Mountains, He Winds Up High

In 2012, invited by Mr. Awosika, the director of the Nigerian Institute of Oceanography and Marine Research (NIOMR) and the Chairman of the Committee of the Limits of the Continental Shelf (CLCS), the Chinese science expedition ship Ocean One had its 26th voyage at the Nigerian coast for half a month. Edward, from NIOMR went to the trip and worked with the Chinese scientists. The voyage made a new record in the Nigerian marine geological and geophysical study and also ferried Edward to China.

At the beginning, Edward had no idea about China or Hangzhou. His only knowledge about the city and the country came from his communications with the Chinese scientists in the half-a-month work. This aroused his curiosity for this big oriental country. Everything seemed to be destined. When the Chinese government offered the marine scholarship, Edward chose to apply for further study in China. This unexpected opportunity just came at the right moment. On September 2, 2013, Edward registered at Zhejiang University and became an international student.

It was said that it would take a while for the expats to adapt to the new environment, but Edward never felt like a stranger in this city, although he had never been here. The convenient communication also eased his homesickness. After settling down, Edward began taking courses at Zhejiang University and doing research at the Second Institute of Oceanography of the State Oceanic Administration. He studied the sediment dug out by the China-Nigeria joint voyage in the Atlantic Ocean. He would figure out the paleo-climate-and-environment evolution in the Atlantic tropics as recorded by the sediment. He hoped to further improve his scientific research capacity through his study in China and planned to continue contributing to the oceanography studies in Nigeria.

Edward's instructor, Professor Han Xiqiu, is a marine expert. Professor Han values teaching and group work. She would organize weekly seminaries for her students to discuss their research progresses. As everyone studies a different topic, Edward learned a lot and was greatly inspired. The group meeting system and the teamwork spirit were his favorite part in his study.

Professor Han Xiqiu is concerned about her students as well as being strict with them. She is rigorous and meticulous in the research. As for Edward's papers for publication, Professor Han would correct word for word, again and again. She thinks besides research capability, it is important to improve the students' scientific writing habits. "Research papers have to be revised many times before they are up to publishing."

In the past few years, Edward was given many opportunities, such as attending a series of academic conferences. From April 22 to 23, 2014, Edward went, on behalf of the SIO, to the Fourth International Symposium on Scientific and Legal Aspects of the Regimes of the Continental Shelf and the Area held in Xiamen; From September 25 to 27, 2015, he went to Nanjing to attend the Third International Symposium of Mid-ocean Ridge Theory; On October 28, 2017, he gave the presentation titled "Deep sea turbidites from the abyssal basin of eastern Equatorial Atlantic" on the 6th National Sedimentological Congress.

When Edward was in poor health, Professor Han Xiqiu, bought him a blood pressure monitor for him to carry about. In Nigeria, Edward's income was medium high, barely enough to support his two children to school and his big family for a living. During his study in Zhejiang University, Edward's scholarship covered his tuition fee, dwelling, and medical insurance, plus 3,700 yuan allowance per month. Professor Han gave him an extra 1,400 yuan monthly allowance so that Edward had some savings to send back home to support his family.

In 2014, jointly organized by Ministry of Natural Resources of China and Zhejiang University, Edward visited the Great Wall and the Forbidden City in Beijing. He spent a long time on the Great Wall trying to remember this world wonder as much as possible.

Edward had never thought that China could be in such a great order despite of its huge population—the busy yet tidy streets, the convenient and cheap public transportation, and the highly accessible roads and subways. His classmates were very warm and friendly. Enthusiastic and cheerful as he was, he would talk to the passengers on the bus, making friends with them. If anyone asked to add him to the WeChat friends, he would usually accept.

Meticulous in science, yet the love between Professor Han and her students was strongly bound. Professor Han used to publish in her WeChat moments a picture of a bottle of snacks that Edward brought from his hometown as gifts to the group.

His time in China was a lifelong memory. Edward brought home his knowledge and his capacity of doing research as well as the friendship and love. He was sure about his future, confidently and firmly serving for the oceanic study. He was lucky to have a good opportunity of studying in a good environment from a good instructor. He worked hard and he reached the most of his expectations. He was grateful for what he got, "thanks to the Chinese government and to my professor and to the team who helped me so much. "May Edward pursue his dream in the future as much as he did in China.

当倒计时声起，在不舍之外的那些

　　留学生的故事时常从一个朴素的想法开始——国外的某门学科或领域发展得很好，自己很向往，希望去成就自己的学业和学术梦想。

　　他们中的一些行动派，放弃在故乡已拥有的稳定生活，选择出国留学，在短短几年的时间里，经历跨国、跨界的多重考验。几乎每段看起来很美的留学故事，都曾有过艰涩的开端。

　　敞开的中国大门，包容开放的浙江大学，吸引着越来越多的留学生到这里继续深造。2015年，塞缪尔——一个带着想法、怀有志向的尼日利亚年轻人，选择来到中国深造，那是因为同单位的一些前辈们在浙江大学的亲身学习经历与体验深深地吸引着他，他也想到浙江大学攻读博士学位，不断提升自己的价值。

　　在向自己的工作单位——尼日利亚国家海洋研究所提交留学申请时，他精心准备了计划书，与14名同事竞争到中国留学的机会。通过评选委员会的严格评审，他幸运地被选中。刚入学时，塞缪尔不曾接触过自己将要研究的领域，因此，他的起步相较于其他同学要困难些。

　　刚来到中国的第一年他是在浙江大学度过的。他渴望知识，多选修了几门课程。起步不易，但"勤能补拙"，塞缪尔深谙其道，他反复告诉自己，周围都是聪明且好学的同学，自己必须付出更多才能赶上。在第一年的基础知识学习中，他每天保持着18小时的高学习强度。除了平时的上课时间和周末留给自己购置生活用品的时间，他通常待在自习室，每天从早上睁开眼睛持续到夜晚，学习"分秒不休"。他经常自习到凌晨，别人早都歇下了，但他还在啃课本、读文献。这份毅力着实让人感叹，而他的刻苦也并非一时的热情，直到现在，他也坚持每天学习不低于12小时。

一年以后，塞缪尔来到自然资源部第二海洋研究所（以下简称海洋二所）韩喜球课题组参与科研。尚未见到韩教授时，塞缪尔就了解到韩教授严于把

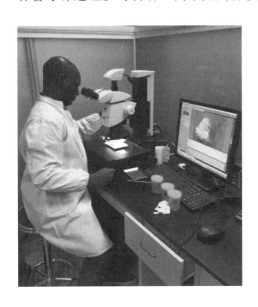

关，对自己的学生要求很高，这对于一个本来就用功刻苦的人来说，更是一份额外督促自己保持上进的动力。即便是日后，师生之间熟悉了，但在对待科研上他们也没有丝毫的马虎。

塞缪尔在海洋二所实验室
Samuel in the lab of the Second Institute of Oceanography under Ministry of Natural Resources of China

在导师的影响下，塞缪尔一直相信，"成功没有捷径"。他是一个实干家，显著进步的背后是每天的分秒必争。塞缪尔的努力都被导师看在眼里，韩喜球教授说他"好学、踏实，接受能力也很好，所以进步很快"。汗水的积累使得塞缪尔的知识面得到极大拓展，他现在研究的主要方向是印度洋洋中脊热液沉积作用。在研究过程中，他接触到多种精密的科学设备，如电子探针(EPMA)、扫描电子显微镜(SEM)、X射线衍射分析等。在尼日利亚时，他从未想过自己能亲手使用这些精密仪器设备来分析样品。得益于浙江大学先进的图书馆系统和丰富的文献资源，塞缪尔经常通过阅读最新的高层次论文来提高自己的思维和研究能力。甚至是远在尼日利亚的老同事，也常常让塞缪尔帮忙查找文献。

在最近三年里，塞缪尔得以多次参加学术会议，并多次作口头报告：第

三届国际洋中脊理论研讨会（the 3rd Mid-Oceanic Ridge Conference）、第八届全国成矿理论与勘探研讨会（8th Session of National Symposium on Ore-Forming Theory and Prospecting）、第一届江浙青年地球科学论坛（the 1st Jiangsu-Zhejiang Youth Forum on Geosciences）……能参与到这些学术会议，了解到学术热点，并与专家互动提问，一方面拓展了塞缪尔自身的视野，另一方面，同行所提的中肯建议对他的研究有着很大的帮助。尽管他目前的研究区域位于印度洋，但通过研究所积累的经验和认识包括自身科学素养的提升，是可以今后一生受用的。特别是，这方面的研究在尼日利亚还没有开展，因此塞缪尔很高兴，期盼在回到故乡后能发挥更大的作用。

在科研之外，塞缪尔受到了方方面面的照顾。塞缪尔每月可以领取到2000元的浙江大学奖学金，韩教授也为他额外提供了每月2000元的生活费，相对于塞缪尔在尼日利亚工作时每月约相当于1600元人民币的工资收入，这是很大的资助。其间塞缪尔曾回家了三个月，在这段时间里，对他的资助依然是照常发放的。谈起这些，塞缪尔总是止不住地感谢。塞缪尔自知目前所取得的进步离不开导师的长期指导和帮助，对于韩教授，他一直怀着既感激又崇敬的心情。到现在，他的梦想也依然保持着初踏上中国大地时的那份纯朴，只是更明确

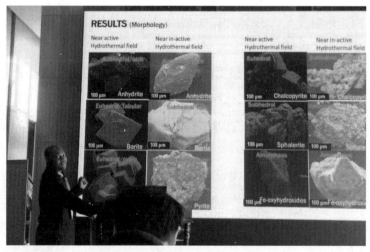

塞缪尔在第八届全国成矿理论与勘探研讨会上作报告
Samuel giving a speech on the 8th Session of National Symposium on Ore-Forming Theory and Prospecting

塞缪尔与参加IODP培训的师生合影
Samuel with the teachers and students after the IODP training

些——成为像韩喜球教授那样的杰出科学家。

　　塞缪尔至今仍然记得自己第一次深切感受中国文化的情景。在与其他同学和老师一起聚餐时，他发现总是由席间的最年长者先动筷，举杯共饮时晚辈的杯子也会略低于长者的杯子，后来他明白了这些举动是出于礼貌和对长者的敬重。"最初我感到很奇怪，但后来就会觉得这是一种体现尊重的极好方式。这些文化以及它们的表现形式是非常有趣的，显示着一种伟大的秩序感。"

　　倒推回刚到中国那会儿，塞缪尔对筷子的认知还停留在中国电影《蛇形刁手》中。起初他还抱怨筷子难以使用，一段时间下来，他出乎意料地发现用筷子吃饭更为简单方便。在这种浓重的文化氛围里学习，他说自己很享受。

塞缪尔与韩教授实验室的团队成员一起
Samuel with the team members of Professor Han's lab

现在，塞缪尔距离毕业只剩下一年的时间，他的妻子届时会从尼日利亚专程来参加他的毕业典礼。他们想在毕业典礼上共同向导师致谢，导师是他前进路上的领路人，给过的帮助和指导太多太多。对于接下来为时不久的留学日子，塞缪尔说他会更加珍惜，因为想学的东西还有很多很多。之后他要回到尼日利亚原先工作的单位，将在中国接触到的文化、所学的知识传播到故乡，推动尼日利亚的海洋研究。

"科研""故乡""文化"，是留学生们口中的高频词汇，他们用自己的努力，在多方的支持下，展示出更多彩、美好的可能。对塞缪尔来说，一年、两年、三年、四年……丰富起来的不仅是知识阅历，也是他的人生。

采访人：张鸿乾

采访日期：2018年4月

When Time Ticks Out, He Becomes Retrospective

The stories of studying abroad often start with a simple idea—a discipline or research field develops so well in another country that the students yearn for fulfilling their academic dreams.

Some of the studying-abroad students simply give up their comfortable life in their hometown to study abroad. In just a few years, they experienced multiple transnational and border-crossing tests. Almost every seemingly beautiful story had a harsh beginning.

Zhejiang University, just like the country under the opening policies, attracts more and more international students. In 2015, Samuel, a young Nigerian with ideas and ambitions, chose to come to China for his further study when fascinated by some of his colleagues' experiences at Zhejiang University. He also dreamed of studying as a doctorate candidate at Zhejiang University for self-realization.

When applying to the National Oceanographic Research Center of Nigeria where he worked, his proposal outstood from the 14 colleagues for the opportunity of studying in China. He was lucky to win after rounds of evaluations. When he first came, Samuel had no knowledge about his research field. Therefore, he was faced with more challenges than other students.

In his first year at Zhejiang University, He was so eager to learn that he registered a few more courses than required. Samuel knew that it was the hardest to make the first step. He repeatedly told himself that practice makes perfection. Surrounded by so many smart and hard-working students, he had to work harder to catch up. In the whole year of basic knowledge learning, he maintained a daily 18 hours of intensive learning schedule. Except for the usual classes and the weekend trips to buy his own daily necessities, he would stay in the classroom learning unceasingly day and night. In the early morning hours, when the whole world was asleep, he still stayed up, reading and studying. His astonishing perseverance and hard working were not impulsive but long lasting. He still studies for no less than 12 hours every day.

A year later, Samuel came to the Second Institute of Oceanography under Ministry of Natural Resources of China (hereinafter referred to as SIO) and joined Han Xiqiu's research team. Before meeting Professor Han, Samuel had been told that Professor Han was strict with

her students. To a hard-working student as Samuel was, this became his dynamics to work even harder. Later, when he became familiar with Prof. Han, he never changed his earnestness to his research.

Influenced by Prof. Han, Samuel does not believe in any shortcut to success. His daily efforts resulted in the remarkable progresses. Professor Han Xiqiu was aware of his endeavors and commended that he was inquisitive, absorbing, and fast growing. All the sweating was paid back in terms of his growth in his study. In his research on the hydrothermal deposition of the mid-ocean ridge in the India Ocean, he was exposed to a variety of sophisticated scientific equipment such as electron probes (EPMA), scanning electron microscopy (SEM), and X-ray diffraction analysis that he never thought about using when in Nigeria. Thanks to the advanced library system and the abundant literature resources at Zhejiang University, with the access to the latest high-level papers, Samuel improved himself in thinking and in doing research. Some of his colleagues back in Nigeria also had him help searching documents.

In the past three years, Samuel went to quite a few academic conferences and did presentations: the 3rd Mid-Oceanic Ridge Conference, the 8th Session of National Symposium on Ore-Forming Theory and Prospecting, the 1st Jiangsu-Zhejiang Youth Forum on Geosciences... In these academic conferences, he learnt about the academic focal points, interacted with experts, broadened his vision, and found help for his research. Although his was studying the Indian Ocean, the experience and understanding accumulated in it as well as his research capacity would benefit in his lifetime. Particularly, since there are no similar researches in Nigeria, Samuel will be more achieving after returning home.

Beyond the research, Samuel enjoyed a wonderful treatment in all aspects. He had a Zhejiang University scholarship of 2,000 yuan per month. Professor Han also provides him another 2,000 yuan monthly allowance. Compared to his 1,600 yuan monthly salary in Nigeria, it was a good income. In addition, he was still paid when he went back home for a three month vacation. Samuel was all thanks for the supports he got and for Professor Han. He attributed his progresses to her constant guidance and help. He had the same dream as he first came to China, but his target became clearer—to become a scientist as eminent as Professor Han Xiqiu.

Samuel still remembered his first experience in the Chinese culture. While having dinner with his classmates and teachers, he found that Chinese people would have the most respected person start eating first and would lower their glasses when having a toast with an elderly person. Later he realized the etiquette behind it. "I felt strange at the beginning, and then realized that it was a good way to show the respects. The culture and the way people practice it are very interesting. It is a great sense of social order."

When he first arrived at China, Samuel's cognition of chopsticks was gained from Jackie Chan's movie *Snake in the Eagle's Shadow*. At the beginning, he complained about the difficulties of using chopsticks, but surprisingly he soon found it easier and more convenient. He enjoyed his full immersion in the special culture.

Today, Samuel has only one year left before his graduation. His wife will come to his commencement. They hope to thank Professor Han at that special moment. As his leader in his study, she has given him so much help and guidance. Samuel said that in the rest days of his stay he would make the most of this opportunity. After going back to Nigeria, he would introduce the culture and knowledge he has learned in China to his people and would promote the marine study in Nigeria.

Research, hometown, and culture are the frequently used words among the international students. With the help from multiple parties, they strived to perform perfectly. For Samuel, the few years studying abroad had enriched his knowledge, experience, and his life.

学问无遗力，工夫系国情

"学问无遗力，工夫系国情。"这10个字是留学生妮莫的真切写照。她是来自柬埔寨的环境部工作人员，她的到来，承载着柬埔寨环境部对学习先进海洋环境知识的期盼；她的学业，紧系着当地未来海洋污染治理的国情。

赤潮：问题紧迫，一拍即合

作为柬埔寨的一名环境部人员，妮莫已经工作了将近一年半。妮莫所在部门的工作目标是管理和保护生物多样性，促进自然资源的正确使用，从而实现柬埔寨的可持续发展与长远利益。她在那里主要负责研究活动和收集科研以及社会数据，从而为这些环境问题找到原因、影响和切实可行的解决方针。

这段时间，妮莫亲眼见证了柬埔寨愈发频繁的环境问题。生物多样性的减少、不可持续的非法采伐和捕捞、生态系统的退化和生物多样性的栖息地的改变，一桩桩、一件件令她十分痛心。她心里始终有一个遗憾，那就是自己不能够以科学的方式和优异的学识素养，来应对遇到的这些环境问题。她希望成为一名优秀的科学家，为国家的发展做出终身贡献，用自己的科研助力解决国家甚至世界范围内的环保问题。

2016年，柬埔寨沿海爆发了这个国家有史以来的第一次赤潮，当地的海洋渔业和水产资源受到了极大的破坏，给当地居民的健康也带来了威胁。柬埔寨

完成环境管理和保护短期课程后H. E. Say
Samal给妮莫颁发了证书
Nimol awarded by H. E. Say Samal
after taking the short-term course of the
environment management and protection

环境部从未遇到过类似的问题，对于如何应对一筹莫展。作为一个在海洋环境
保护方面刚刚起步甚至还算不上起步的国家，柬埔寨在这一方面目前只相当于
我国20世纪五六十年代的水平。柬埔寨的环境部立刻意识到了问题的紧迫性，
并开始采取措施向其他在海洋治理方面更加成熟的国家和组织寻求帮助，积极
地参与世界各地的交流与培训。

在一次国际海洋环境相关的学术会议上，柬埔寨海岸带环境部部长H. E. Say
Samal和中国国家海洋局国际合作司处长冯军交流了柬埔寨国内海洋环境保护
落后、缺乏海洋专业人才的问题，得知中国政府的海洋奖学金项目，H. E. Say
Samal向冯军推荐了妮莫。他们对妮莫到中国的学习充满希冀，期盼她能在这
里学到先进的知识与海洋治理经验，回国后为本国的海洋环保出一份力。

这样一个契机，为妮莫开启了浙大海洋学习的新篇章。在来到浙大前，妮
莫正在德国参加由德国和日本组织的关于环境保护的23个发展中国家培训班。
一结束，妮莫就马不停蹄地从德国直接来到了中国，开始了海洋生物专业的研
究生学习。在获得了这次实现志向的机会后，她时时提醒自己不仅要学习知
识、掌握知识，更要带回知识、应用知识。

科研：心系国情，潜心学业

妮莫毕业于柬埔寨最好的大学之一——金边皇家大学，有着不错的学习基
础。更重要的是，妮莫的学习热情和学习决心十分强烈，这让她在学习科研中

受益匪浅。妮莫在以前的学习中从未进行过化学分子实验，因此在这一问题上犯了难。她便主动和有经验的同学一起去实验室。同学在了解到妮莫的困惑后，也主动为她细致地解释分子实验中的每一个步骤与重点，令她受益匪浅。在和浙江大学海洋学院博士生导师佟蒙蒙的交流上，妮莫也十分积极。在每周一次的组会上，她会将自己的疑惑与需要和导师交流。平时一旦遇到问题，她也会及时寻求老师的帮助与指导。"老师为我的课程与研究提供了非常丰富的资源与细心的指导，任何时候我遇到学业问题，我都可以有人咨询。"妮莫十分感谢这里的老师和同学。

妮莫凭借着积极的态度和勤奋的付出不断努力着，使得自己在浙大的学习逐渐顺利起来。妮莫的导师佟蒙蒙称赞道："虽然她可能缺失一定的实验工作基础，但是她了解知识、接受知识的能力是非常不错的。"

目前妮莫的学习与研究内容与她的国情息息相关。柬埔寨在海洋环境治理上，尤其是在有害藻华应对上面的空白始终是她心里放不下的问题。她担忧地说道："在过去的十年里，有害藻华在全球范围内急剧增加，它们可能对海洋生物、水质、人类健康和海水淡化厂造成危害。而这其中的原因主要是人类活动增加了海洋生态系统的压力。"

为了能更好地参与以后的环保工作，她正在修习海洋生物、海洋生态、海洋微生物等关于海岸带管理方面的课程，并将有害藻华爆发后的海岸带管理作为自己主要的研究方向。在佟蒙蒙导师的指导下，妮莫开始了关于亚太经合组织（APEC）国家有害藻华爆发后管理的研究与调查，在其他国家的应对案例中总结经验、寻求突破。

妮莫发现，现在的科学家们已经可以在赤潮等事件发生之前预测事件，并发送预警信

妮莫（左2）参加2017年APEC研讨会
Nimol (left 2nd) in the 2017 APEC seminar

号。她坚信，在可期的未来人类不仅可以提供灾害预报，而且还可以在它爆发之前采取措施将其抑制住。

有了在中国的科研学习与经验借鉴，她对祖国治理海洋问题的未来充满信心。

缘分：渊源不浅，文化亲近

妮莫与中国有着十分深厚的缘分。

同为亚洲人，妮莫的长相与中国人十分相似，若是不说话，恐怕大多数人都会将她看作一个中国姑娘。在来到中国的这段时间里，妮莫常常被校园里的同学或者路上的行人当成中国人。她笑着说："时常有同学会直接用中文和我进行交流，当听不懂中文的我解释了自己的留学生身份后，对方才恍然大悟。这真是非常有趣的误会。"

在柬埔寨，妮莫所属的这一家族支系，回溯源头还有着中华民族的一缕血脉。她和家人们在很多风俗习惯上和中国十分相似，比如说许多中国的传统节日，他们也会一起庆祝。

兴许是因为这些缘由，妮莫对中国的方方面面都有着骨子里的亲近与喜爱。在假日里，妮莫经常会骑着自行车外出游玩。她最喜欢秀美温婉的西湖。中国便利快捷的公共交通和移动支付使她印象颇深。以前的她还从未有过这样的出行体验。"这里的道路上随时可以看到各种各样的公共交通，从公交车到公共自行车，甚至还有公共的电动自行车。而且我出门不再需要携带现金，只要有我的手机，就可以支付一切，哪怕是街头的小吃摊或者小餐馆！"中国紧跟时代的生活方式与便民利民的公共环境都着实让妮莫赞叹。

妮莫在杭州西湖边留影
Nimol by the West Lake in Hangzhou

妮莫在上海参加2017中国政府海洋奖学金留学生游学活动
Nimol on the trip with the 2017 Marine Scholarship winners

现在的妮莫，也燃起了学习中文的兴趣。她会通过手机向同学们咨询中文问题，或者向身边的校园服务人员寻求帮助。周围乐于助人的友好氛围，不仅让妮莫在生活学习上少了很多困难，还给了她更多了解中国文化的机会。她非常喜爱中国的早餐，尤其是这里的包子和粥。"虽然我的国家也有这些食物，但和这里的完全是不一样的风味，所以我每天都会去食堂吃早餐"，妮莫这样介绍道。

舟山的冬天很冷，来自热带的妮莫生活上虽有不适应，心里却很温暖。在漂亮洁净的校园中，在井然有序的图书馆中，在香气氤氲的食堂中，在气氛融洽师生和睦的实验室中，她一点点亲近中国、融入中国、爱上中国。

海洋学院图书馆是进行文献综述的最佳和最舒适的地方
The library of Ocean College——the best place for literature reviewing

采访人：陆理宁

采访日期：2018年3月

Try My Best to Study for My Country

"Try my best to study for my country." This is indeed how Nimol is like. As a staff of the Cambodian Ministry of Environment, with the ministry's longing for the advanced marine environmental knowledge, she came to China studying a major closely related to the future marine pollution management in Cambodia.

Red tides: Pressing issue requiring a quick decision

Nimol has worked for her present position for almost a year and a half. Her department manages and protects biodiversity to ensure the proper use of natural resources and the country's sustainable development and the long-term benefits. Her research is to collect the scientific and social data so as to figure out the causes to the environmental problems, as well as their consequences and solutions.

During her stay, she witnessed the ever more frequent environmental problems in Cambodia, the decrease of biological diversity, unsustainable and illegal logging and fishing, as well as the degradation of ecosystem and the shrinking of biodiversity habitats. Such changes made her heart-broken. She wished to be able to deal with such problems with scientific methods and excellent knowledge. She longed to be an outstanding scientist, contributing to her country in her lifetime and solving the domestic or even worldwide environmental problems.

In 2016, marine red tides broke out in Cambodia for the first time, damaging the local marine fisheries and aquatic resources, posing a threat to the public health. The Cambodian Ministry of Environment not having encountered the problems of the kind, knew nothing about how to deal with it. In terms of the ocean environmental protection, Cambodia was as clueless as China was in the 1950s and the 60s. The Cambodian Ministry of Environment realized how urgent it was and began to take measures by seeking for help from the countries that were advanced in marine environment management and by getting actively involved in exchange and training programs worldwide.

At an international conference of marine environment, the Cambodia minister of environment H. E. Say Samal and the director of the international department of China's

Ministry of Natural Resources of China, Feng Jun, discussed Cambodia's challenges in environmental protection and in marine professionals training. When H.E Say Samal learned about the Chinese government marine scholarship, he recommended Nimol to Feng Jun. The young Cambodian had high expectations for her learning in China, hoping that she could learn some advanced knowledge about the ocean and its management so as to contribute to her country after returning to Cambodia.

For Nimol, this was a brand new chapter in her marine studying. Before coming to Zhejiang University, she was in a training program in Germany organized by the German and Japanese governments for 23 developing countries. As soon as she finished that, she started her study in the ZJU graduate program. She kept reminding herself to study hard for her country.

Doing research—to her country, she devoted herself

Nimol graduated from one of the top universities in Cambodia, the Royal University of Phnom Penh. A good student as she was, her passion and determination for learning also benefited her in doing research. One of the challenges she encountered was the chemical molecular experiment, of which she had no previous knowledge. She sought help from the experienced students, having them do the experiments together and explain to her every detail and key point. She was also active in the seminars held by her instructor Professor Tong Mengmeng from the Ocean College of Zhejiang University. In weekly meetings, she would communicate with Professor Tong about her doubts and her wants. "My professor gave me abundant resource and guidance. She's so helpful that whenever I have difficulties, I would ask her for advices." Nimol was grateful for getting to know Professor Tong and her classmates.

Her constant efforts, positive attitudes, and hard work made her study in Zhejiang University more and more enjoyable. Professor Tong praised Nimol "competent in learning and understanding despite of her lacking previous experimental exercises."

Nimol's present study and research are closely related to Cambodia's national conditions. The country's deficiency in marine environment management, especially in harmful algal blooms worried her immensely: "In the past ten years, the more and more frequent occurrence of harmful algal blooms worldwide may do harm to marine lives, water quality, human health, and the desalination plant. Human activities brought about more pressures on the marine ecosystem."

In order to do a better job in the environmental protection in the future, she registered classes relative to coastal zone management, such as the marine biology, marine ecology, marine microorganism, etc., and chose post-harmful-algal-bloom coastal zone management as her major research. Under the instruction of Professor Tong, Nimol did the research and investigation into how the Asia-Pacific Economic Cooperation (APEC) countries dealt with the harmful algal blooms, seeking for a breakthrough from the cases of these countries.

Nimol found that scientists were able to predict red tides and send warnings ahead of time. She had faith that human beings could not only forecast the disaster, but also take measures in advance.

She was very confident with Cambodia's ocean management after learning in China.

Destiny: The two cultures are always close

Nimol seems to have her destiny to China.

She looks so much like a Chinese that before she speaks she is frequently taken as a Chinese. Such mistakes occurred so many times in and out of the campus that she was amused by how she made people surprised when she claimed that she didn't understand a word of their Chinese. "It was always fun to see how dumbfounded they were learning that I'm a foreigner," said Nimol.

Nimol's family has a wisp of Chinese heritage if dated back to her ancestors. The family even has similar customs to the Chinese ones, say, they celebrate many Chinese festivals together.

Perhaps such family traditions made Nimol close to the Chinese and love China. In holidays, she would ride a bicycle to tour around the West Lake She liked the convenient and fast public transport and the mobile pay. She said she had never experienced such outings before. "Here all kinds of public vehicles can be seen everywhere, from buses to bicycles, even the electric scooters. Plus, no cash is needed. With my cell phone, I can buy anything anywhere, even street food!" She was amazed by the modern lifestyle and the convenient public environment in China.

Nimol developed a strong interest in learning Chinese. She asked questions to her friends in Chinese and sought for help from the campus service. The friendliness of the strangers and the friendship of her friends helped her out from difficulties and taught her a lot about the local culture. Her favorite part of the culture was the breakfast, especially the dumbaozi and

porridge. She explained, "we have food of the same kind in Cambodia, but the flavor is totally different. I would go to the cafeteria for breakfast every day."

Winter is cold in Zhoushan. Coming from a tropical area, Nimol was not used to such cold weather. But all the warmth from the friendly people counteracted it—on the beautiful and clean campus, in the clean and tidy library, in the warm and savory cafeteria, and in the laboratory with friendly teachers and students. Nimol found herself fit into and fall in love with China little by little.

情在浙里，缘系两地

从红海之滨到东海之畔，从厄立特里亚到舟山，这个年少时就热爱自然、关心环境的非洲小伙儿一路走来，从食品工程学到海洋科学，一次又一次地书写了自己与中国的美好故事——他就是正在浙江大学海洋学院攻读海洋资源与环境博士学位的留学生博汉。

博汉（左1）在江南大学获得硕士学位
Berhane（left lst）being awarded his Master's degree certificate at Jiangnan University

漂洋过海的二次情缘

事实上，来浙大读博不是博汉的第一次中国之行。在厄立特里亚的阿斯马拉大学读完本科后，博汉当了两年中学教师。凭借自己对教育的热情和抱负，他获得了在位于马萨瓦的海洋科学与技术学院担任助教的机会。在兢兢业业地工作了三年后，博汉的努力没有被辜负，政府选派他到中国进修，到江南大学攻读食品发酵工程专业的硕士学位。在三年在华学习的时光里，博汉渐渐适应了中国的生活，结交了许多中国朋友，也爱上了这个古老的国度，他带着不舍和眷恋离开了这里，却没有想到自己与中国的缘分还不止于此。

2017年，厄立特里亚政府与中国政府有了新的合作，博汉看到了再次回到中国深造的可能性。经过和同事们激烈的竞争，博汉凭借优异的表现脱颖而出，获得了中国政府奖学金国别双边项目的支持，开启了自己的第二次中国之旅。初到舟山，这个美丽的岛屿立刻吸引了博汉。"这里的环境很整洁，非常安静，适合想居住在临海地区的人，海鲜还很好吃啊。"而六个月的浙大生活也让博汉越来越庆幸自己能来到这所中国顶尖的高等教育学府，很幸运能在这里遇到自己的导师。在博汉眼里，浙江大学海洋学院是一个非常适合想钻研海洋科学的人的地方，他将浙大形容为"学习海洋科学的最佳选择"，而学院所有的课程和科研教学都与他的学习目标不谋而合，这使他对未来的学习与生活充满期待。

如今已是博汉在中国的第四个年头，他时常会笑着说："我感觉自己现在像个中国人了。"面对陌生的环境和随之而来的问题，博汉从未畏惧，而是选择正面去处理这些事情。即便是在初到中国、中文并不熟练的时候，他就已经敢于说中文，时时想着要鼓起勇气尝试着去说，加之性格十分外向，博汉很快有了很多的中国朋友，而和他们用中文交流也成了博汉最喜欢做的事情。久而久之，博汉的中文越来越好，对中国文化和习俗的了解也越来越深入，可以说是留学生中的"中国通"。来到舟山后，开朗的博汉自然和实验室的同学们相处得很融洽，他很快就交到了新朋友，同时也期待着能在这里结交更多的中国朋友。

二度漂洋过海来到中国，博汉与"浙里"的故事才刚刚开始。

"感觉能做，就决定去做。"

2015年，在中国获得硕士学位的博汉回到了厄立特里亚的海洋科学与技术学院任职。而这一次，他渐渐注意到毗邻的红海除了印象中的美丽和壮观之外，开始出现了一些海洋问题。随着工业化和城市化的发展，预防或解决海洋生态环境问题刻不容缓，而这也成了博汉想要研究的一大方向。他想从改善自己国家的海域状况开始，努力学习研究解决水体问题的方法，最终能为全球水体治理做一点贡献，而这也是他来到浙大的目标和动力。

现如今的博汉已经在海洋生物研究所的佟蒙蒙老师和海洋二所曾江宁老师的指导下定好了初步的博士学位研究方向，制订了自己的研究计划，进入了博士研究生正式的科研阶段。博汉将目光聚焦在海洋酸化、有害赤潮、海洋生态和海洋浮游植物等核心课题上，学到了许多如有害微藻研究等在厄立特里亚接触不到的内容，并将所学知识与对红海的研究结合了起来。面对全新的知识，博汉十分珍惜浙大给予的学习和实践机会，还在导师的带领下参加了几个研讨班。无论是2017年的"APEC海洋空间规划和海洋保护区管理培训"还是第三届IOC中国—非洲海洋科技论坛，博汉都代表学院和自己的国家，分享了关于海洋科学研究的想法，介绍了自己对红海的了解，指出了其中的海洋问题，得到了不错的反馈。在这两个

2017年博汉在第三届IOC中国—非洲海洋科技论坛上演讲
Berhane giving a speech at the 3rd IOC China-Africa Forum on Marine Science and Technology

博汉与佟蒙蒙老师团队成员在一起
Berhane with the team members at Professor Tong Mengmeng's lab

高标准的研讨班中，博汉学到了很多以前不了解的知识，受到了专业的指导。同时，这对博汉来说，也是一个向大家介绍厄立特里亚的平台。在增进双方对彼此的了解的同时，博汉更明白了自己将来能为中厄合作做些什么，也对推进两国的合作有了更大的信心。

而博汉能快速地融入浙大的学习环境，自然与他和导师间融洽的关系密不可分。

在海洋生物研究所的佟蒙蒙老师眼中，她带的学生博汉是一个挺特别的留学生——他是刚进实验室就能上手做科研的"极少数"。有了在中国获得硕士学位的基础，个人能力很强的博汉成了实验室的留学生里上手最快，也是最优秀的学生。热情的博汉凭借自己扎实的学科基础，在实验室里给其他留学生充当起了半个"导师"的角色，辅助老师更好地将信息传达给其他留学生。这个经验丰富的"师弟"成了几个留学生的"领头羊"，促进整个实验室一起学习、一起进步。

在博汉的心中，他的两位导师有着举足轻重的地位。每当他产生一个想法，佟老师和曾老师都很乐意给他提供帮助和建议，而正是有了他们的指导与支持，博汉的一个个想法才有可能变为现实。博汉是一个随时准备好接受挑战的学生，也绝不会轻言放弃，

博汉（右）与曾江宁教授参加2017年APEC研讨会合影
Berhane（right）with Professor Zeng Jiangning in the 2017 APEC seminar

因而遇事都有自己的计划，但他更喜欢将自己的计划和导师们的建议融合起来。当导师们强调一些观点和建议时，博汉总是能快速地理解，他总是告诉自己："感觉能做，就决定去做。"

博汉相信人都会遇到困难，重要的是如何去解决它们。在最开始接触微藻时，他有着诸多不明白的地方，但在佟老师告诉他要跟紧相关研究时，他就努力地去学习、去攻破，而在老师的帮助下，事实上研究也进展得非常顺利。这份自信与坚持让博汉突破了一个又一个学习上的难关，让他一步步地向自己的目标不断前行。

剪不断的纽带

将博汉与中国紧紧联系起来的，不仅是两国政府间的合作，还有一份关乎人、关乎文化的情。

博汉至今还记得自己第一次见到佟蒙蒙老师的场景。他来到了佟老师的办公室，佟老师热情而友善地接待了他。那时的博汉正面临选课难题，苦于不知道该如何操作选课系统，而佟老师让博汉坐下，亲自指导他选完了所有的必修课。博汉惊讶于佟老师的体贴与耐心，而在之后的相处中两位导师更是如家人一般给予他关心和帮助。博汉觉得中国和厄立特里亚一样，都是和平而纯净的国度，中国人民的热情好客令人尊敬，而这样的亲切感也加深了博汉与中国的情谊。

博汉作为留学生代表主持了海洋学院2018年的新年晚会
Berhane hosting the 2018 New Year's Party of Ocean College as a representative of the international students

在学习之余，乐于尝试新事物的博汉还作为留学生代表主持了海洋学院2018年的新年晚会。这对博汉来说，不是一件很容易的事情。第一次登上舞台，第一次在这么多人面前说中文，第一次紧张地在后台练习唱《茉莉花》，在一个个"第一次"中，博汉与浙大的关系又近了一步，与中国文化又近了一步。2018年，他还代表浙大留学生登上了舟山当地的电视台，在新春佳节给中国朋友们拜了年，这些难忘的回忆都让博汉与中国建立起了剪不断的纽带。

辗转间已是在华求学的第四个年头，博汉一次次地往返于中国和厄立特里亚之间，用学识为两国搭建起了一座桥梁，为了共同的保护和探索海洋的目标而不断努力。谈及未来，博汉希望能顺利地完成博士学位要求的所有研究课程，在毕业后回到厄立特里亚，尽己所能，将在中国学到的知识传递给家乡的年轻人，带领他们服务和回报祖国，致力于提高国家的教育水平。同时，他希望毕业后能保持和两位导师的联系，在已有合作的基础上，共同开展对红海的研究，开展更多更深入的科研合作。他希望自己能成为连接中国和厄立特里亚的纽带，推进两国进一步的合作，彼此信任，携手同行。

采访人：徐奕宁

采访日期：2018年3月

2018年博汉参观海南三亚猴岛
Berhane visiting the Monkey Island in Hainan in 2018

2018年博汉在海南三亚实地采样
Berhane sampling at Sanya, Hainan in 2018

Love in Zhejiang University

From the Red Sea to the East China Sea, from Eritrea to Zhoushan, from fermentation engineering to ocean science, the young African PhD student at the Ocean College of Zhejiang University, Berhane Teklehaimanot Tesfai, who loves nature and cares about the environment, has created his stories in and with China again and again.

His second trip to China

In fact, it was not Berhane's first visit to China when he came to Zhejiang University. After completing his undergraduate studies at the University of Asmara in Eritrea, Berhane taught in a secondary school for two years. With his enthusiasm and ambition for education, he got the teaching assistant position in the College of Marine Science and Technology in Massawa, Eritrea. After three years of hard working, his efforts were paid off when he was chosen to continue his higher education abroad by the government of Eritrea. He was sent to Jiangnan University in 2009 studying fermentation engineering. There, he got his master's degree in 3 years. During this period of time, Berhane got used to his life in China, made many Chinese friends, and fell in love with this ancient country. He left with great reluctance, not knowing that his stories with China didn't stop.

In 2017, the Eritrean government had a new cooperation with the Chinese government. Berhane saw the gleam of returning to China for further studies. Thanks to his outstanding performance, Berhane gained the Chinese government marine scholarship after the fierce competitions against his colleagues. With the support of this China-Eritrea bilateral program, Berhane came back. When he arrived in Zhoushan, he was immediately attracted by the beautiful island, "The clean environment, the friendly people, fresh seafood, and the peaceful life here make it a dream place for those who like to live close to the ocean." After six months of living at Zhejiang University, Berhane felt fortunate to study in a top institution in China and fortunate to meet his professor. As Berhane emphasized, the Ocean College of Zhejiang University is a place perfect for the students and researchers who hope to do something in marine science. He described Zhejiang University as "the best choice for learning marine science." The curriculum and research plan of the college went perfectly well with his research

goals. This made him long to his future.

Berhane had been here for about 4 years. He would often claim: "I feel like I'm a Chinese." In the face of challenges in new places, Berhane never feared, but chose to deal with them positively. When he first arrived in China, he could speak no Chinese and was innocent in the culture, but he took every opportunity to practice the language. Attributed to his outgoing and open-mindedness he made a lot of Chinese friends pretty soon. Talking with them in Chinese became Berhane's favorite moments. As time went by, Berhane spoke more and more Chinese and knew better of the culture. After coming to Zhoushan, the cheerful Berhane got along very well with other students in the laboratory. He quickly made some new friends and he also looked forward to making more Chinese friends here.

The story of Berhane and ZJU had just begun.

"When I feel like I can do it, I just do it."

In 2015, Berhane, returned to the Eritrea College of Marine Science and Technology with his master's degree that he got from China. This time, he gradually noticed that beautiful as it was, the Red Sea began to have some ocean problems. With the growing industrialization and urbanization, it became imperative to prevent or solve marine ecological problems. Berhane decided to study Marine Science for his PhD. He wanted to play a role in protecting and managing the water environment by learning how to deal with the upcoming challenges of marine environment. To contribute to the Red Sea marine environment, as well as the global one motivated him to come to Zhejiang University.

Currently, under the guidance of Professor Tong Mengmeng and Professor Zeng Jiangning, Berhane has pinched down his general research direction for his PhD, finished the outline of his research plan and started working on it. Berhane focused on such core issues as ocean acidification, harmful algal blooms, marine ecology, and marine phytoplankton. He learned many recently hot topics such as harmful microalgae which he included in his own research. This is totally new to Eritrea. Berhane cherishes the learning and practicing opportunities at Zhejiang University. He followed his professors to attend several seminars. In 2017, in the APEC Marine Space Planning and Marine Conservation Area Management Training Program and on the 3rd IOC China-Africa Forum on Marine Science and Technology, Berhane, on behalf of the College and his country, shared his ideas on marine science research, introduced his understanding of the Red Sea, and pointed out the problems of the ocean. His presentations were well recognized. In these high-end seminars, Berhane learned a lot of previously unknown knowledge and received professional guidance. At the same time, he found it a good chance to introduce his beloved country, Eritrea. While enhancing the mutual understanding between China and Eritrea, Berhane figured out more about what he could do for China-Eritrea cooperation and how to do it.

Talking about Berhane's immersion into the new environment at Zhejiang University, his professor, Tong Mengmeng, has to be mentioned.

Professor Tong works at the Institute of Marine Biology. Her impression on Berhane was "a very special foreign student." He was among the "very few" students who could do research once in the laboratory. With his previous experience of learning for his master's degree, Berhane soon became one of the top students in the laboratory. He even acted as a part-time tutor for the other international students, assisting his teacher to better communicate with them. This experience made him a leader among the international students, creating an atmosphere of learning in the laboratory.

According to Berhane, his two professors are very important. Whenever he had a new idea, both Prof. Zeng and Prof. Tong would be willing to help and give him advices. Berhane's ideas couldn't be realized without their guidance and supports. Berhane is always ready for new challenges and never gives up. He seems to have plans for everything, but he prefers to integrate his professors' advices into his plans. He has a good perception of his professors' points and suggestions, thus, he usually urges himself: "If I can do it, I just do it."

It is natural that everyone has difficulties in his life. But according to Berhane, how to deal with them is more important. When he first learnt about phytoplankton (microalgae), there were a lot of contents that he didn't know about. But when Prof. Tong told him to keep up with the latest research results, he worked really hard to learn and to break through. With Prof. Tong's help, his study turned out very well. With the self-confidence and perseverance, Berhane broke through the difficulties in his learning one after another, moving forward step by step toward his goals.

Inseparable ties

Berhane's ties to China were not only built up by the governmental cooperation, but also by the love for and from the people and the culture.

Berhane still remembered his first meeting with Professor Tong Mengmeng in her office.

Although he had never met her, he was kindly treated and welcomed. When he inquired about the online class registering system, Professor Tong helped him out step by step. Berhane was very moved by her patience and thoughtfulness. She was one of the two professors who guided him academically and treated him like family. They made him realize that China is like Eritrea, peaceful and traditional and that the Chinese people are amazingly hospitable.

Berhane loved to try new things. On the 2018 New Year's Party of Ocean College, he served as a representative of foreign students and became one of the hosts of the party. That was not easy for him. It was his first time hosting on the stage, first time speaking Chinese in public, and first time singing "Jasmine" (*Mo Li Hua*), a Chinese classical song. In all such first trials, Berhane became more indulged in the life at Zhejiang University and in the local culture. This year, he starred in a New Year show on behalf of the Zhejiang University international students on Zhoushan television. These unforgettable memories have made an inseparable tie between Berhane and China.

Berhane went back and forth between China and Eritrea in the four years studying, bridging the two countries with his knowledge in the joint pursuit for the protection and exploration of the sea. Talking about the future, Berhane hoped to finish all the required courses for his doctorate degree, and to return to Eritrea after graduation. He hoped to teach the young people when he goes back, guiding them to serve the country and to improve the country's education. At the same time, he hoped to keep touch with his two professors to continue their research and to seek for new cooperation opportunities. He hoped that he would be a strong tie between China and Eritrea, so as to promote further cooperation between the two countries and work for a mutually benefited future.

她的征途是星辰大海

"在我第一次在沿西印度洋中国—莫桑比克联合航次的船上遇到唐勇教授的那一刻前,我从没想过自己有一天能来到浙江大学学习,"屏幕那端,晓楠露出了略带羞涩的笑容,中英文夹杂着将她一路走来的故事娓娓道来,"能来到中国,遇到这一切,我是幸运的。"晓楠是Nelta David Matsinhe的中文名,晓楠特别喜欢这名字。

相隔万里,风雨兼程

莫桑比克和中国之间相隔了近万公里,对于很多人来说,跨国留学是需要深思熟虑的。然而,在晓楠看来,这只是一瞬间的决定而已。谈起和中国的缘分,晓楠显得格外激动,迫不及待地向我回忆起了当时的情景。

"2016年,由于参加了由中国自然资源部第二海洋研究所和莫桑比克海洋内水渔业部国家渔业研究所之间进行的沿西印度洋中国—莫桑比克联合航次,我有幸成为参与中莫联合航次在莫桑比克海峡进行首次考察的6名莫桑比克籍科学家之一。真的很感谢这次机会,让我结识了来自海洋二所的唐勇教授和他的团队。这次野外实践经历对我决定未来在海洋地球科学领域继续追求我的学术和职业生涯有很大影响。"据晓楠说,在这一次科研合作中,她从地震勘探船上的中国籍科研工作者那里收获了许多知识与经验,而这些都是她在莫桑比克学习时未曾经历过的。"我发现，中国科学家的知识与经验得益于政府的支持和鼓励。而这在大多数非洲国家并不现实，因为这些国家缺乏在科研上的资金投入。同时，我也惊异于中国学生们在此次地震研究中所展现的技能和专业知识。由此，我萌生了到中国去学习的想法。"

据了解，晓楠当时所在的这一航次，是中国和莫桑比克实施"南南合作"的重要体现。此次合作深化了各方对东非典型被动大陆边缘构造演化的认识，密切了两国海洋研究机构和专家间的合作关系，提升了中国海洋科研调查工作在非洲的影响力，其重要性可见一斑。就这样，在这艘非同寻常的"向阳红10号"船上，在西印度洋海面粼粼波光的见证之下，晓楠与中国的缘分徐徐拉开了序幕。

2016年晓楠（左6）有幸参与中莫联合航次
Nelta(left 6th) on the Sino-Mozambique expedition in 2016

令晓楠难忘的时刻——首次将海底地震仪（OBS）部署到海洋以采集数据
Unforgettable moment to Nelta—deploying the OBS to the ocean for the first time

"晓楠来自非洲。刚认识时她有些腼腆，在相处过程中我慢慢发现她是一名非常优秀的青年。她勤奋、刻苦，对于不懂的问题很有刨根问底的精神。"当被问及在航次合作过程中对晓楠的印象，唐勇教授表示出了极大的赞许。"莫桑比克方也对她期望很大，希望晓楠能对莫桑比克南部大陆边缘构造加强理解，提高科技水平，深化对区域的认识。学成后回到祖国，在国内建立和中国的联合研究中心。"

在唐勇教授的介绍和晓楠的自述中，那次初遇的情景似乎就在眼前。而我也仿佛看到了晓楠，一个勤奋自强的女留学生，正克服着包括文化差异、语言障碍等重重困难，从熟悉的莫桑比克来到陌生的舟山，毫不犹豫、斩钉截铁地开启了全新的生活。

跨越重洋，只为追寻自己心中的梦想。而这个梦想关乎海洋、成长和远方。

正如她自己所说："这里的一切和我家乡完全不同，说没有困难是不可能的。不过，好在我的家人非常支持我，我也能在更好的平台上研究自己热爱的领域。因此，我从未后悔。"那么，既然选择了远方，便只顾风雨兼程。

潜心科研，学有所长

"我的地球科学学术生涯始于2012年，当时我决定申请到蒙德拉内大学进行地质学的学习和研究工作，那是一所在莫桑比克历史最悠久、规模最大的大学。"晓楠出生于莫桑比克马普托市，是家中最年长的孩子。在来到浙江大学之前，她已经获得了地质学学士学位。

谈及自己会选择研究地球科学领域的原因，晓楠坦言道："在莫桑比克，主修工程学课程和地质学课程的女性很少，这是因为在我们传统观念中女性不擅长也不能胜任与这类专业相关的工作。比如，在大学里，有35名同学跟我一起上地质学课程，其中女同学还不到10个。"晓楠紧接着解释道，由于近些年在莫桑比克盆地发现了油气藏，国家对地球科学的专业人才才有了更多的需求。也正因为如此，现在她故乡的许多女性才有机会在这个领域进行学习和研究。未曾附庸风雅，亦不趋之若鹜，只追求一种单纯的喜欢和理想。就这样，晓楠在她所热爱的领域坚定地走了下去。

"我高中毕业后就开始申请大学，用我的科学知识为祖国发展做出贡献是我的人生目标之一。正如前面所说，我打算从事地球科学方面的研究以帮助国家发展。但遗憾的是，我们国家没有足够的研究条件帮助我在这个领域做更加深入的研究和探索。幸运的是，我遇到了唐勇教授，并得到了来浙江大学读研的机会。"目前，晓楠正在浙江大学海洋学院攻读海洋地质学硕士学位，主要研究莫桑比克大陆边缘地质、深部结构、外大陆架划界问题。

谈起在中国和莫桑比克学习上的最大不同，晓楠表示，这体现在日常科研生活的方方面面。"我知道浙江大学是中国最好的大学之一，在这里学习和在我祖国的学习经历非常不同。这里有更昂贵的高科技仪器、更先进的理念、更大的平台，而最重要的是我在这里遇到了李老师。"

李春峰老师是晓楠在浙江大学的合作研究生导师，在学习生活方面都给予了她很大的帮助。"李老师是一位非常负责任的教授，他总是为我们准备好一切。他不仅仅是导师，更像是一位好朋友。"提及自己的导师，晓楠的脸上浮现出感激的笑意。"我刚来到中国半年，人生地不熟，李老师总是我遇到困难时最先想到的人。"

而提起自己带的留学生，李春峰老师脸上同样有藏不住的笑意。"晓楠面对学习和科研时那股专注的劲头，是连我都忍不住钦佩的。我非常希望她可以在这里学有所成，今后继续攻读博士，回国后成为相关领域的专家，起到学科带头作用。"

尽管如此，先进的科研环境和暖心的导师依然不能为初来乍到的晓楠铺平所有道路，有些困难注定要自己一个人去经历和克服。"对我来说，最难的是语言关。我在莫桑比克的母语是葡萄牙语，因此，英语和汉语都需要不断加强和练习，"晓楠如是说，"但无论如何，我的学习生活非常美好，没有理由抱怨科研学习的辛苦。因为对于我们海洋地质学领域的留学生而言，浙江大学已经是一个很好的学习和研究的平台，在导师和同学们的帮助下，我开始为我在中国学习期间想要进行的研究工作制订计划。浙江大学海洋学院设立的交流项目，也让我们更多地融入中国人的日常生活之中。这一切都是我非常感动和感激的。"

始于热爱，终于理想

如今，晓楠来到浙江大学舟山校区学习已有半年之久，她依旧能清晰地回忆起第一次来中国时的感受。"我被中华文化的博大精深深深吸引了，那一刻我觉得，这便是我想要生活与学习的地方。"中国是一个拥有古代文明的多民族国家，与莫桑比克一样，在信仰、服饰、饮食、语言、艺术方面都有其独特底蕴。这种多样性，代表了中国的文化和历史。同时，对龙的形象及意义的好奇，也激发了晓楠对中国的更多向往。"我想要更加深入地了解这个美丽的国家。"

当被问起最喜欢中华文化的哪一部分时，晓楠腼腆地笑了："我最喜欢的？那一定是吃了！因为中国的食物实在是太美妙了。"由于住在舟山，平时接触海产品较多，晓楠无可救药地爱上了吃海鲜，同时也喜欢吃一切辣味菜肴。谈起这些时，晓楠俨然变身为一位热爱生活的美食家，津津乐道她对中国菜的喜爱。

除美食以外，晓楠对生活的许多方面都抱有满腔热情。她热爱游泳、健身，更像许多非洲姑娘一样能歌善舞。据唐勇教授所说，在沿西印度洋中国—莫桑比克联合航次的航船上，晓楠大展歌喉，凭借一

2017年晓楠入学时正遇浙江大学120年华诞
At the 120th anniversary of ZJU in 2017 when Nelta was enrolled in the university

晓楠游览杭州西湖
Nelta visiting the West Lake in Hangzhou

首泰坦尼克号主题曲摘得了歌唱比赛桂冠。在舟山校区，她也参与了元旦晚会的舞蹈表演，翩翩舞姿给全场观众都留下了深刻的印象。对晓楠而言，科研是生活的底色，而这些丰富的爱好就如同星辰洒满夜空，散落在她学习生活的一点一滴之中。

采访的最后，我询问了晓楠硕士毕业后的规划，谈起未来，她的眼中散发出了无限光芒。"众所周知，一个国家需要通过科研来提高自身发展的潜力。因此，我毕业后的计划是回到莫桑比克，与祖国的人们分享在中国的留学时光和学到的知识。毫无疑问，我坚信，凭借着从浙江大学获得的知识，我可以成为大学或研究机构里一位出色的地质学研究员，并继续研究莫桑比克大陆边缘。"

晓楠还表示，她打算把大陆边缘的构造演变及其矿物资源相关研究领域作为博士研究课题，并希望可以建立一个海洋地球科学领域的平台，通过这个平台向莫桑比克学生讲授地球科学知识，同时也为中国和莫桑比克的科学家创造沟通交流经验的机会。"我相信这可以让更多像我一样的学生有机会获得知识，也能对莫桑比克海洋地球科学研究的发展做出贡献。我们美丽的莫桑比克大陆边缘在海洋资源方面有很大的潜力等着我们去发掘和探索！"在这头头是道的阐述、逐渐清晰的规划之中，我仿佛看到了一颗海洋地球科学界的新星，正冉冉升起在我的面前。

访谈接近尾声，晓楠似乎还依依不舍，意犹未尽。在她的建议下，我们互相交流了在各自语言文化中表达爱意的方式。看着她一笔一画地在纸上写下葡萄牙语的"我爱你"，并放慢语速说给我听，我猛然意识到，此时在我面前的远不仅仅是一位优秀而卓越的未来女科学家，更是一位对生活充满热爱的年轻姑娘。而来到中国，来到浙江大学，只是晓楠梦想之船扬帆的起点。这一路纵使要披荆斩棘，乘风破浪，也在所不惜。而支撑她一路走来的，是心中那份对海洋科学研究的热忱，和对祖国无法割舍的爱。朝阳于海面冉冉升起，梦想之船即将起航，而她的征途，是星辰大海。

采访人：王迎晓

采访日期：2018年3月

Embrace the Ocean

"When I first met Professor Tang Yong on the ship of the China-Mozambique joint voyage in the Western Indian Ocean, I never thought that one day I could study in Zhejiang University (ZJU)."At the other end of the screen, the slightly bashful Nelta smiled. Slowly her story began to unfold through her impeccable English. "I have been lucky to come to China and experienced everything." Nelta has a Chinese name Xiao Nan, which she likes very much.

Journey across the oceans

Mozambique and China are nearly 10,000 kilometers apart. For many, studying abroad is something to ponder. However, in Xiao Nan's view, it was just a split-second decision. Talking about her predestination with China, Xiao Nan seemed to be particularly excited, and couldn't wait to tell me what happened at that time.

"In 2016, after participating in the China-Mozambique West Indian Ocean voyage, jointly organized by the Second Institute of Oceanography under Ministry of Natural Resources of China and National Fisheries Institute under Ministry of Marine and Inland Water Fisheries of Mozambique, I became one of the six Mozambique scientists who had been to the first Sino-Mozambique expedition in the Mozambique Channel. I am really grateful for this opportunity. On this trip, I got to know Professor Tang Yong and his team from the Second Institute of Oceanography. This field experience had a great impact on my decision to pursue an academic and professional career in the field of marine geoscience in the future."According to Xiao Nan, during this research collaboration, she learnt a lot from the Chinese researchers on the seismic survey ship, which she had never been to while studying in Mozambique. "I found that the Chinese scientists are benefited from the government support and encouragement. That was not the case in most African countries due to a lack of state funding. At the same time, I was also impressed by the skills and expertise shown by Chinese students on this trip. Therefore, I came up with the idea of coming to study in China."

It was learned that the voyage that Xiao Nan went on was an important embodiment of the "South-South Cooperation" between China and Mozambique. The joint study was of great significance in deepening the understanding of both parties on the tectonic evolution of the typical passive continental margin in East Africa, boosting the collaboration between the two countries' marine research institutions and experts, and enhancing the influence of China's marine scientific research in Africa. Witnessed by the sparkling Western Indian Ocean on the special ship of "Xiangyanghong 10", Xiao Nan's predestined tie with China started to forge.

"Xiao Nan was a bit shy when I first met her. But gradually I found that she was an excellent young woman—diligent, hard working, and inquisitive." When asked about his impression on Xiao Nan during the joint voyage, Professor Tang gave her a big thumb-up, "the Mozambican side has high expectations for her, hoping that she could strengthen her understanding of the continental margin of Southern Mozambique, improve her research capability, and enlarge her knowledge in this field, so that when she returns after graduation, she can play a major role in setting up a joint research center with China."

The narrations of Professor Tang and Xiao Nan brought us vividly to the scene of their first meeting. And I could almost see how Xiao Nan was like—a diligent and self-reliant student, striving hard to overcome the difficulties, in the culture and in the language. But leaving behind her familiar homeland for the totally strange Zhoushan to start a new life, she showed no hesitation.

She came across the ocean to pursue her dream, the dream about the ocean, about her growth, and about the distant land.

As she put it herself, "Everything here is so different from that in my hometown. I will not be telling the truth if I say there are no difficulties. However, my family is very supportive and I can study my favorite field on a better platform. So I have never regretted it." Having made the choice of going to a distant land, she will endure all the trials and hardship.

Dedicated to her study and research

"My academic career in geoscience began in 2012 when I decided to apply to study and research in geology at Mondlane University, the oldest and largest university in Mozambique." Xiao Nan was born in Maputo of Mozambique and is the eldest child in her family. Before coming to ZJU, she had received a bachelor's degree in geology.

Speaking about why she chose to study earth science, Xiao Nan confessed: "In Mozambique, there are very few women majoring in engineering or geology due to the tradition that women are neither good at nor competent in the work related to these fields. In college, for example, 35 of my classmates took geology lessons with me, and less than 10 of them were women. Xiao Nan explained that the country has a higher demand for geoscience professionals because of the discovery of oil and gas reserves in the Mozambique Basin in recent years." That's why many women in her hometown now have the opportunity to study and research in the field. She was not chasing fashion or trend, but only to pursue a simple liking and ideal that Xiao Nan treads firmly down the path of her choice.

"I started applying for college education right after graduating from high school. It was one of my life goals to contribute to the development of the nation with my knowledge. As stated earlier, I intend to pursue research in earth science to help my country grow. Unfortunately, it does not have adequate research conditions to allow me to do more in-depth research and exploration in this field. But fortunately, I met Professor Tang Yong and got the chance to attend the graduate school in ZJU." At present, Xiao Nan is studying for her master's degree in marine geology at the Ocean College of ZJU, focusing her study on the geology of the Mozambican Continent margin, its deep structure and the demarcation of its outer continental shelf.

Talking about the biggest difference between Chinese and Mozambican studies, Xiao Nan believes it is reflected in every aspect of daily research life. "I know ZJU is one of the best universities in China, and the learning experience here is very different from that in my motherland—more expensive high-tech instruments, more advanced concepts, bigger platforms, and most importantly, getting to know Professor Li. "

Professor Li Chunfeng is Xiao Nan's graduate instructor for her cooperative research program in ZJU, and has been very helpful in both her study and life. "Professor Li is a very responsible professor who sees everything ready for us. He is not only an instructor, but more like a good friend." Referring to her instructor, Xiao Nan smiled gratefully. "I have just been in China for half a year and am unfamiliar with the place and people. Professor Li is always the first one who comes to my mind when I run into difficulties."

Mentioning the overseas student under his instructions, Professor Li Chunfeng could not help smiling, either. "I am really impressed by her dedication to study and research. I sincerely hope that she can finish her program here and continue to study for a PhD later. I also hope she will be an expert and play a leading role in the discipline."

Nevertheless, the advanced research environment and the warm-hearted instructor could not clear everything off her way when she first arrived. Some difficulties are just inevitable. "The toughest thing for me is the language barrier. My native language in Mozambique is Portuguese, so both my English and Chinese require constant reinforcement and practice."

Xiao Nan said. "But anyway, I truly enjoy the study life here, and have no reason to complain the hardship of research. For us overseas students in marine geology, ZJU is a super learning and research platform we can hope for. With the help of my tutor and classmates, I began to make plans for the research work I need to do during my study in China. The exchange program set up by the Ocean College of ZJU helps our integration into the daily life of Chinese people. For all these, I honestly feel very touched and grateful."

Her passion and ideal

By now, Xiao Nan has been studying in Zhoushan campus of ZJU for half a year. She can still clearly recall her feelings when she first came to China. "I was fascinated by the depth and breadth of Chinese culture, and at that moment I felt that this is where I want to live and learn." China is a multi-ethnic country with an ancient civilization. Like Mozambique, China has its unique heritage in terms of belief, costume, food, language and art. Such diversity represents the Chinese culture and history. At the same time, Xiao Nan's curiosity about the image and significance of the dragon also inspires her yearning for China, "I want to know more about this beautiful country."

When asked which part of the Chinese culture she likes best, Xiao Nan grinned bashfully, "My favorite? That must be the food! Chinese food is just fabulous!" Living in Zhoushan, the country's largest fishing ground, Xiao Nan has hopelessly fallen in love with seafood and also taken to all kinds of spicy dishes. She seems to have become a real foodie, talking on end about her fascination with the Chinese meals.

Apart from the delicious food, Xiao Nan is enthusiastic for many things in her life. She loves swimming, working-out, and is good at singing and dancing like many African girls. According to Professor Tang, Xiao Nan won the singing contest with a song from the movie *Titanic* during China-Mozambique joint voyage on the Western Indian Ocean. On Zhoushan campus, she danced as a performance at the New Year's party and stunned the audience with her graceful movements. For Xiao Nan, scientific research is the texture of her life, while her interests and hobbies are like the patterns decorating it.

At the end of the interview, I asked Xiao Nan about her post-graduate plans. Talking about the future, her eyes lit up. "As is known to all, a country needs to improve its development potential through scientific research. I plan to return to Mozambique and share my experience and knowledge learnt in China with my people. Undoubtedly, with my

experience at ZJU, I can be a good geological researcher in a university or research institute. And I shall continue my research on Mozambique Continent margin."

Xiao Nan also said that she is going to take the tectonic evolution of the continental margin and its mineral resources as her PhD research subject so that she can set up a marine geoscience platform, via which the lectures on geoscience knowledge can be accessible to Mozambican students, and the Chinese and Mozambican scientists can communicate with each other. "I believe this will give more students like me the opportunity to acquire knowledge and contribute to the development of marine geoscience research in Mozambique. The Mozambique's continental margin has the great potential in marine resources for us to explore and uncover!" The clear and logical plan depicted a rising star in the future marine geosciences for me.

Before ending, Xiao Nan seemed to be reluctant to leave. As she suggested, we exchanged the ways of expressing love in our native language and culture. As she carefully wrote down "I love you" in Portuguese on a piece of paper and read them slowly to me, it struck me that the girl in front of me was more than just a brilliant scientist-to-be but a young lady full with love for life. Coming to China and ZJU is just the starting point of Xiao Nan's dream. Her passion for marine science and her love for her country drove her march forward.

While the sun is rising on the sea, her dream boat is about to set sail to fulfill her great ambitions.

亦坚亦远的学术之心

尤娜的人生旅程是蓝色的，是与海洋相伴的。这片海，是她的家乡——毛里求斯的摇篮；这片海，是她远道而来、筑梦浙大的缘起；这片海，是她探索知识、勇攀学术高峰的天地。

她跨海而来，怀揣着一颗亦坚亦远的学术之心。坚，是她全心科研的专注；远，是她不畏漫途的勇气。

怀学术热情，筑梦浙大

尤娜与浙大的相遇是一次机缘巧合。

尤娜的家乡是被誉为印度洋上三颗明珠之一的毛里求斯，是一个美丽的热带海岛国家，海岸线有两百多公里。与海洋缘分深厚的她，获得了生物学的本科学位，又修习了与海洋环境相关的硕士学位。在环保部任职期间，尤娜对于海洋环境保护的相关知识有了一定的了解，继而产生了在海洋环境方面继续深造的念头。

与此同时，一个奖学金项目为她的梦想添了一份力，坚定了她的想法。中国政府设立了一系列奖学金项目，以资助来华留学生在中国高校和研究机构进行学习和研究，进一步加强中外的友谊与合作，中国政府海洋奖学金就是其中之一。拥有海洋学习背景和出色环保工作经历的她毫无疑问成了毛里求斯政府推荐给这一项目的合适人选。

尤娜的导师浙大海洋学院博士生导师肖溪教授讲述了她与尤娜在一次共进晚餐时听说的故事。"那时的尤娜需要在两个选择中做出决定，一个是和她当时任职的环保部续约稳定且很有前景的工作，另一个是告别亲人离乡背井远到浙江大学求学，而这两个选择刚刚好撞在了同一天。"权衡再三，尤娜最终还是选择了自己内心对学术科研的热爱与追求，来到了中国深造。

她坚信，这不仅是学术上提升的好机会，也能够为她日后回到国内、将知识与才能应用在毛里求斯海洋环境保护与开发等各领域铺好道路、打好基础。肖溪导师为尤娜的决心与志向深深触动："即便是在中国，在拥有了家庭和事业之后，仍选择全身心地投入学术科研也是极其需要勇气的，而远在毛里求斯的尤娜能够做出这样的决定更是极为可贵的。"

融文化之差，收获友谊

而今的尤娜说，这是一个给她带来了极大惊喜的选择。无论是浙大完备丰富的体育设施、新奇有趣的宿舍生活，还是在国内外卓著的学术声誉、可提供的科学研究和发表论文的机会，都让尤娜愈发地庆幸自己当时的选择，对浙大的热爱也渐渐植根于心。她笑着说："不管别人如何评价这所学校，浙大在我心里都是最棒的！"

作为一个体育迷，尤娜喜欢游泳、骑自行车、打羽毛球、打乒乓球等各种运动，浙大舟山校区的体育场馆里时常有她

尤娜喜欢在舟山校区游泳池游泳
Yuvna in her favorite swimming pool of Zhoushan campus

尤娜（左1）与同学在舟山校区田径场
Yuvna (left 1st) with her classmates at the playground of Zhoushan campus

挥洒汗水的身影。"这里有非常大的恒温泳池和很棒的羽毛球场，工作人员们也将设施维护得很好。"本科和硕士阶段都是走读制的她还在这里第一次体验了宿舍生活。她喜欢和室友们在浙大为学生准备的毕至居①中一起做饭、一起聚餐、一起开派对。她对自己在浙大交到的第一位中国朋友记忆颇深。"他是我在实验室里的同学硕士生李超，他不仅帮助我在这里安家，为我来回地搬行李，还带我去附近的超市购置生活用品，让我很快地安顿下来，适应了浙大生活。"这份在浙大收获的友谊，成了尤娜宝贵的财富。

来自热带国家的尤娜起初在生活习惯上遇到了一些问题，她不好意思透露。由于生活习惯不同，刚来到这里的她总是赶不上食堂的饭点。但很快地，在同学和老师的帮助下她努力调整自己的生活步调，渐渐适应了这里的用餐时间。对于浙大舟山校区的饭菜，尤娜赞不绝口："我很喜欢中餐，学校的菜品也很丰富，尤其是舟山的海鲜料理非常美味！"

"浙大是一个非常适合文化交融的好地方，我在这里充分地见证了不同文化、不同民族之间的交往与融汇。"她还利用空闲时间游历中国的各式风景，从上海的霓虹璀璨、高楼林立到杭州的山明水秀、温柔雅淡，尤娜见证着中国的别样魅力。如果说尤娜是一条活泼的鱼儿，那中国就是她自由徜徉的大海。

---

① 宿舍楼里为学生提供的可以做饭的地方。

与导师相伴，攻坚克难

异国他乡的学习在尤娜和肖溪教授之间搭起了一座桥梁，两颗心随之越走越近。这也难怪，同是年龄相仿的已为人母的女性，自然不乏共同话题。采访中，尤娜和肖溪老师十分亲密，笑声不断，仿佛就是一对异国的好姐妹。无论是学术上的问题，还是诸如买生活用品的这类生活琐事，尤娜都乐于与导师交流，导师也悉心回应。肖溪教授发自内心地称赞道："这么漂亮，聪慧，比一般同学还要更加开朗的尤娜也给我带来了太多的意外！"

在采访的间隙，尤娜饶有兴致地问起了肖溪导师目前的妊娠近况，和她谈起了两个国家产假时间的差异。肖溪导师开玩笑说，虽然产假有好几个月，但她生完孩子一个月后就会照常地来"监督"尤娜的科研进程。两位亦是师生、亦是姐妹的亲密友谊不仅来源于尤娜开朗热情的性格，更离不开肖溪导师在学术和生活上真心相待的付出。

尤娜印象最深的是来到浙大的第一个中秋节。中秋月圆，丹桂盛开，在这个中国人讲究合家团圆的节日里，留学生们却刚刚远离家乡，远离亲人和朋友。肖溪老师不忘这些从异国来此的留学生们，也想给初来中国的他们留下一个美好的回忆。于是把自己的家人从杭州接到舟山，和留学生们一起用一个厨艺聚会来共度佳节。善厨艺的老师和留学生们每人都带来了菜肴，尤娜不善厨

导师肖溪老师（左3）和同学们为尤娜举办欢迎晚宴
Her classmates and Prof. Xiao Xi (left 3rd) holding a welcome party for Yuvna

艺，便开心地为同学们和导师打下手。她称赞道："那天的海鲜和菜肴让我非常难忘！"一旁的肖溪老师打趣道："那你还记得我那天做的蒸螃蟹吗？"

除了和尤娜成为生活上的朋友，肖溪老师亦是学术上的严师。每周一次的学术组会、科研进程的进度汇报……研究海洋环境的尤娜和本科学习环境工程的肖溪教授在学术上十分契合。肖溪教授开授了一门中文课——海洋环境保护，尤娜对此很有兴趣，可是却在语言上遇到了困难。肖溪教授知晓后对她开放了这门课程，并专门为她准备了英文的学习资料，还在授课的PPT上加入了许多英文内容，为尤娜带来了极大的方便。尤娜说，这是她来到浙大后上的最喜爱的课程之一，是肖老师带给了她如此珍贵的课程体验。

浙大如家，尤娜在这里拥有了珍贵的同学友谊与师生情谊，同时她也在这里享受到了家庭之乐。就在采访的这段时间，尤娜的丈夫也利用假期来到了舟山陪伴妻子，和她一起游玩学习。尤娜还打算明年将自己的儿子接来中国度假，让他也体验一下中国的文化。

展自信气度，书写人生

严谨的学术氛围、开放的发散性思维、完善的实验设施，在这样的环境中，尤娜全身心地投入到海洋科学的研究之中，将科学研究与环保实践相结合，书写自己的学术篇章。她目前主要的研究内容是大型海藻养殖对海洋环境的影响。这项研究不仅具有很高的工业价值，还能开发出多种活性物质用于生

尤娜参加第三届中非海洋科技论坛
Yuvna at the 3rd China-Africa
Forum on Marine Science and
Technology

物制药。更为重要的是，它在人类应对气候变化方面有很大的借鉴意义。

她提到了自己研究的一种海藻——江蓠。"这种藻类对于解决近海海水的富营养化有很大作用，可以吸收水体中多余的矿物质盐，从而为其他水产的养殖提供更加洁净的水体环境。"当谈起自己的研究时她神采飞扬，眼底满是憧憬与希冀。

到浙大后，她凭借着极强的学习能力与适应能力，很好地融入了这里的科研学习。谈到这里的课程与科研，尤娜露出了自信的笑容。"因为我的学习背景，所以我能够很好地掌握这里的课程。而且在科研方面，我也十分相信自己的能力，无论是文献上的研究，还是投入实验，我都能做得很好！"目前，尤娜还在学习中文，这也是她掌握了英语、法语、印地语等语言之后的第六门语言。她分享了自己学习中文的小窍门："汉语是我遇到的和以往语言很不一样的一种语言，汉字是我遇到的一个难题，所以我在遇见新字新词后会立刻记录下来反复复习。当然，我觉得拼音是汉语的基础，只有掌握好拼音才能更好地交流！"

尤娜的自信与开朗，宛如毛里求斯海岸边明亮耀眼的太阳，在浙大舟山校

尤娜在第三届中非海洋科技论坛上做报告
Yuvna giving a speech at the 3rd China-Africa Forum on Marine Science and Technology

尤娜作为来自毛里求斯的留学生代表参加浙江
大学新年晚会
Yuvna on the New Year's party of ZJU
as the representative of students from
Mauritius

快乐地与同学们在一起
Yuvna with her classmates

区散发出灼灼光芒，感染了她的同学们，也感染了她的导师。目前，她打算继续修习几门课程，首先把课业的学习保证好，而在接下来的两年里就全身心地投入课题组的科研之中。自信和投入是尤娜十分可贵的两个特质，正是有了这两个法宝，尤娜在学习和科研之路上越走越远。

关于未来的学习与生活，尤娜目前有两个计划。一个是在获得博士学位之后，回到祖国毛里求斯的环保部，利用自己在浙大学习积累的海洋环境知识更好地帮助自己的国家，投入海洋保护之中；另一个计划是继续进行博士后的科研工作，把自己的学术科研之路继续下去，走得更远更深。她坦言自己现在还没有做出最后的决定，不过她坚信自己会在日后的科研中找到方向，确定自己未来的人生计划，并一如既往地付出无限的热情与努力。

采访人：陆理宁

采访日期：2018年3月

Commitment with Academics

Yuvna's life is accompanied by the ocean, the cradle of her hometown—Mauritius, the origin of her dream of learning at ZJU, and the field of her learning and research.

She came across the sea, determined in doing research and persistent with it.

With her passion for the research, she came to Zhejiang University

Yuvna learned about Zhejiang University coincidently. Yuvna's hometown, Mauritius, is known as one of the three pearls on the Indian Ocean. It is a beautiful tropical island country with a coastline of more than 200 km. She loves the ocean. She has received her bachelor's degree in Biology and her master's degree in the Coastal Zone Management, a subject of the Marine Environment major. When she worked at the Ministry of Environmental Protection, Yuvna learnt the relevant knowledge of marine environment protection, which in turn led to her pursuit in this field.

At this time, a scholarship program made her dream reachable and made her determined. The Chinese government set up a series of scholarships, aiming to reinforce China's international friendship and cooperation, supporting the international students coming to study and doing research in Chinese universities and institutions. The Chinese Government Marine Scholarship was one of them. With her Marine Science background and outstanding environment protection work experience, she undoubtedly became a suitable candidate recommended by the Mauritian Government.

Professor Xiao Xi, a PhD supervisor at the Ocean College, Zhejiang University, was Yuvna's instructor. She talked about a story she was told at a dinner with Yuvna. "At that time, Yuvna had to make a decision between these two choices—to renew her contract with the Ministry of Environmental Protection, keeping the stable yet promising position, or to bid farewell to her relatives and leave for Zhejiang University to study. The two choices just happened to arrive on the same day." After serious consideration, she finally chose China.

She believed that this did not only provide a good opportunity for academic advancement, but also paved the way for her applying her knowledge and talents to various fields such as marine environmental protection and development upon her return to Mauritius. Professor

Xiao Xi was deeply touched by Yuvna's determination. "Even in China, it requires excessive courage to devote oneself to the academic research after having a family and a business. Taken that Yuvna comes from such a faraway place, her decision is extremely awesome."

Cross-cultural friendship

Yuvna said that her choice brought her great surprises. Whether it was Zhejiang University's fascinating sport facilities and exciting dorm life, or its outstanding academic reputations and the easy access to scientific research and publications, Yuvna became increasingly thankful for her choice, while her love for Zhejiang University became deeply rooted in her heart. She said, "No matter how others comment on this school, Zhejiang University is the best in my heart!"

As a sport fan, Yuvna was good at swimming, cycling, badminton, table tennis and etc. She often did exercises in the stadium. "The huge heated swimming pool and the great badminton court are very well maintained." Living on campus for the first time, she liked cooking, eating, and having parties with her roommates. She remembered very well her first Chinese friend, "He is my classmate named Li Chao. We work in the same laboratory. He helped me move to the dorm, carry my luggage back and forth when I first arrived. He also took me to the nearby supermarket to buy daily necessities. Thanks for his help, I could quickly settle down and adapt to the life here." This friendship upon her arrival had become a valuable asset for her.

Coming from a tropical country, Yuvna had some difficulties with her living habits. At first, she was too embarrassed to ask for help. She was always late for the meals when she first came. But with the help of her classmates and teachers, she adjusted herself and adapted to the schedules pretty soon. Yuvna was very pleased with the food at the Zhoushan campus. "I like Chinese food very much. The food in the school cafeteria is full of varieties. The seafood is extremely good!"

"Zhejiang University is a very good place for cross-cultural communications. I have witnessed the exchanges and integration between different cultures and different ethnic groups." She also spent her spare time travelling across China. From the lights and skyscrapers in Shanghai to the elegant and beautiful landscape in Hangzhou, Yuvna witnessed the unique charm of China. If Yuvna can be compared to a lively fish, then China is her ocean of freedom.

Work with her professors to overcome difficulties

Yuvna and Prof. Xiao Xi became good friends during her stay. Not surprisingly, the two have a lot in common as mothers. In the interview, Yuvna and Prof. Xiao demonstrated how close they were in all the laughter. They were like sisters across the countries. Whether it was an academic puzzle or a trivial perplex in her daily life, Yuvna liked to share with Prof. Xiao. In return, Prof. Xiao responded her with care. "Yuvna, so beautiful, intelligent, and cheerful, has brought me a lot of surprises!" Prof. Xiao commended her sincerely.

In the break of the interview, Yuvna asked Prof. Xiao with interest about her pregnancy. The two talked about the differences in maternity leaves in the two countries. Prof. Xiao teased Yuvna that she would come back to supervise Yuvna's work even in her maternity leave. Their intimacy was partly because of Yuvna's cheerful and passionate personality, and partly attributed to Prof. Xiao's sincerity to Yuvna.

Yuvna was deeply impressed by the first Mid-Autumn Day in Zhejiang University. The bright full moon and the blooming osmanthus made up the picture on this specific festival, a traditional day for family reunions. As the international students were away from their loved ones and friends, they found it hard on such holidays. Prof. Xiao tried to leave them a wonderful memory. She had her family from Hangzhou to Zhoushan in order to spend the holiday with her students. Each of those who cook well brought their special food. Since Yuvna was not good at cooking, she worked as an assistant to her classmates and teachers. "I could never forget the seafood and the other dishes that day." she said. "Do you still remember the steamed crab I made that day?" Prof. Xiao joked at her.

Though being a friend of Yuvna, Prof. Xiao was a strict teacher. She was conscientious on the weekly academic meetings and strict with the reports of her students' scientific researches. Yuvna, who studied the marine environment, was academically geared with Prof. Xiao, who had studied environmental engineering in the college. Yuvna was interested in marine environmental protection, but barred by the Chinese language. Learning about it, Prof. Xiao prepared English learning materials specifically for Yuvna and made her teaching PowerPoint files into bilingual ones. It brought great convenience to Yuvna. Yuvna said that this was one of the wonderful courses that she liked at Zhejiang University. It was Prof. Xiao who brought her such a precious experience.

Zhejiang University was like home to her. Here, Yuvna had met her friends and had the family happiness. During the interview, her husband came to Zhoushan to accompany her and studied together during his vacation. Yuvna also planned to have her son come to China for a vacation in the next year so as to have him experience the Chinese culture.

Live with confidence

With a rigorous academic atmosphere, open-mindedness and perfect experimental facilities, Yuvna devotes herself wholeheartedly to the research of marine science. By integrating her scientific research with her environmental practices, she led a wonderful academic life. Her research was focused on the impact of the large-scale seaweed farming on the marine environment. This research has a significant industrial value as well as a biopharmaceutical value in terms of discovering a variety of active substances. More importantly, it is meaningful for the research into climate change.

She mentioned her research of the seaweed Gracilaria: "it has a great effect on eliminating the eutrophication of offshore waters. It can absorb excessive mineral salts in the water, so as to provide the other aquatic breeds a clean aquatic environment." She was full of enthusiasm talking about her research, her eyes shining with expectations.

At ZJU, Yuvna's complete integration into the research and study can be attributed to her strong learning capacity and her adaptability to the new environment. When it came to her courses and research, Yuvna smiled confidently: "I can master the courses here very well because I'm familiar in this field. I'm confident with my capability of doing scientific research. I can do both literature research and experiments!" Yuvna was still learning Chinese, her sixth language after learning English, French and Hindi, etc. She shared her tips of learning Chinese: "Chinese is very different from the other languages that I have learned. Chinese characters are a major challenge to me. I would keep practicing once I learn a new word. Besides, I think Pinyin is the foundation of Chinese and it's essential to communication!"

Yuvna's self-confidence and cheerfulness were like the bright and dazzling sun along the coast of Mauritius and radiated to the Zhoushan campus of Zhejiang University, warming up her classmates and her professors. At the interview time, she planned to continue to take several courses. Her top goal was to ensure a good performance in her study and then devote herself to the research group work in the following two years. Being confident and devoted were the remarkable personalities that made Yuvna go further on the path of learning and doing research.

As to her future learning and living plans, Yuvna hopes to return to the Ministry of

Environmental Protection of Mauritius after obtaining her PhD., so that she can apply her knowledge of the marine environment she has learned at Zhejiang University to the development of her country and to the marine protection. She also hopes to continue her postdoctoral research work to go further and deeper in her research. She said that she had not made up her mind yet, but she was confident that she would find a direction in her future research. Once setting up the route, she would keep going with the unlimited enthusiasm and efforts as she always did.

精进不休，人生不止

　　半年前，大山还是尼日利亚阿夸伊博姆州大学的一名学术讲师，而现在的他是浙江大学海洋学院海洋工程方向的一名在读研究生。从教师到学生，大山孜孜不倦地追求着更先进、更前沿的知识，并期盼在不久之后将它们带回国内，从而在中国和尼日利亚之间架起一座知识的桥梁。这座桥，沟通的不仅是先进技术，更是对两国未来海洋前景的希冀。

大山在办公室学习
Samuel studying in the office

大山（右）参加海洋奖学金论坛
Samuel (right) in the Marine Scholarship
forum

观实验室，探高精尖

通过声光电技术在陆地上"看见"几千米深海之中的海底热液与珍奇生物是一种什么样的体验？进入到一艘外形时尚、技术先进的200米观光型载人潜水器成为一名"潜航员"又会有怎样的特别感受？远在极地、难得一见的稀有生物们到底长什么模样？这些问题深邃而奇妙，轻轻敲打着海洋科研者的心。

在不久前的中国政府海洋奖学金留学生游学活动中，大山和其他留学生们得到了这些问题的答案。游览同济大学校史馆、深海探索馆，访问上海海洋大学深渊科学技术研究中心、同济大学临港基地、东海大桥和洋山深水港、中国极地研究中心等单位，他们体验了一场难忘的蔚蓝之旅。

中国强大的海洋科考技术与高精尖的深海设备给来到中国不久的大山留下了深刻的印象。而中国海洋技术给他的惊喜，不仅仅在这些博物馆里，也在大山日后即将朝夕相伴的浙大海洋工程实验室中。在浙大海洋学院博士生导师贺治国教授的实验室里，大山看到了许多代表着领域尖端科技的测量仪器，"不仅有测量浊度的LISST、尖端的光学超高速相机，还有专业的锚系设备等，这对我来说是再合适不过的科研环境了！"

这里不仅有强劲的海洋科研实力，更具有容乃大、兼容并包的开放氛围。初来乍到的大山，对一切都不熟悉，但是热情的志愿者们、设备齐全的寝室环境、友好和谐的人际氛围渐渐打消了他对中国的陌生感，使他敞开胸怀了解浙

大山的中国政府海洋奖学金之旅
Samuel on the Chinese Government
Marine Scholarship trip

大、爱上浙大。而大山的足迹也并不止于浙大，虽然才来到中国六个月，他已游历了闻名中外的首都北京、高速发展的都市上海，中国的丰富多元不断带给他新的惊喜。

良师引路，探索方向

舟行海上，迎风而航，大山是知识海洋里的一艘船，那贺治国导师就是指引着他前行的航标灯。在大山的印象中，导师贺治国教授既是一名治学严谨的良师，也是一位心思细致的益友。

还未见到贺治国教授时，满怀好奇与兴奋之情的大山，就通过导师的个人主页查阅了解了不少相关的信息。他查阅到贺治国教授主要从事计算水动力学、泥沙动力学、近海动力过程与海洋工程环境、风暴潮防灾减灾等方面的研究工作，而这正是自己的科研兴趣所在。"我欣喜地发现这位导师不仅有和我十分契合的研究方向，还有许多出色的研究成果与论文，能和贺治国导师一起科研学习是我的幸运。"

"见到他之后，我发现他的确就是我所了解的那样，学识丰富且睿智专业。"而随后的一件小事更让大山对导师的细致用心分外感动。大山未来的科研内容需要进行大量数值计算方面的工作，因此一台合适的科研计算机是必不可少的。贺治国导师担心大山初来乍到、准备不便，就提前为他准备好了计算机，从而方便他到来后可以尽快加入科研，跟上学习节奏。

大山与贺治国教授讨论科学研究工作
Samuel discussing scientific research with Professor He Zhiguo

加入贺教授的课题组进行学习后，大山在生活学习的一点一滴中更加深切地感受到贺治国教授对待学生的耐心负责。"贺老师是一位在我遇到问题时随时都可以寻求帮助和建议的对象。不论是通过邮件和微信，还是去导师办公室直接找他，我总是能十分及时地收到回复。"令大山印象颇深的是，在课题组的微信群中，也总是有着贺教授活跃的身影，他与学生交流着自己科研工作中的经验收获，所见所闻的最前沿研究成果，一点一滴的分享之中都包含着导师的用心良苦。

贺老师治学的严谨认真同样令大山印象深刻，这对他来说，就像科研之路上的警铃，时时敦促着自己。在这位"严师"的指导与帮助下，大山觉得自己能够静下心来更加投入地做科研、做学问。他提到："老师对我们的科研进程抓得很紧，哪怕是在寒假里，老师也会要求我们及时地汇报自己的科研进程，提醒我们做好开学后的计划与展望。"每周一次的例行组会也十分重要，学生们要轮流进行科研进展的汇报与讨论。这对大山来说既是机会，又是挑战。他回想起了自己第一次参加组会时的情景。"那时候我在会上作了自我介绍，阐述了自己的科研想法，我觉得那是我一次很好的自我展示！"大山笑着说。

心系非洲，合作共赢

大山在中国海洋事业的蓬勃发展中，看到了开展双边合作、实现互利共赢的良机。海洋是人类的共同财富，来自尼日利亚的大山也期盼着未来能够与中国科学家一道，为理解海洋、探索海洋、开发海洋做出积极贡献。他时心系非洲，放眼中国，思索着如何能为两国海洋领域的合作出一分力。值得一提的是，"大山"这个中文名，来自于他的中文老师，缘由是著名的中外文化交流使者——加拿大籍学者、主持人大山。或许这其中也蕴含了老师对他日后成为中尼交流使者的期盼吧。

海平面上升是目前国际上的环境难点之一，20世纪以来全球海平面已上升了10～20厘米。这虽然是一种缓发性的自然灾害，但其近年来带来的不良环境影响已经十分显著。一些低洼的沿海地区被淹没，风暴潮强度加剧、频次增

大山的汉语课
Samuel in his Chinese classes

多，大山的家乡——尼日利亚也受到了不可忽视的影响与威胁，这引起了大山持续的关注与担忧。他是个行动派，立刻开始了相关的研究工作。2015年，他就研究了海平面上升对英国沿海地区的影响，并在英国的北威尔士作了学术报告。

不久前，第三届由中国自然资源部第二海洋研究所和浙江大学联合举办的中非海洋科技学术论坛在杭州召开，会议上大山作为课题组的代表发表了关于海平面上升对尼日利亚海岸线影响的报告。他在报告中介绍了海岸线的脆弱性状况，并列举了潜在的影响，提出了沿海管理措施方面的建议。作为一名海洋工程方向的科研工作者，大山深切地认识到海洋环境与海洋开发相关知识对于国家和人民的重要意义。他说，这也是自己来到浙江大学海洋学院这所实力卓著的院校进行深造的原因之一，"这所大学致力于海洋前沿研究，推动了中国乃至世界的许多相关领域的科学创新和技术进步"。

中尼两国在海洋方面的合作由来已久，在2012年中国就派遣"大洋一号"科考船与尼方实施联合海洋调查，开创了中国在非洲国家专属经济区开展海洋科技合作考察的先河。近年来，中尼两国在海洋以及其他领域的合作共赢正在以良好的势头发展着。有了像大山这样的留学生群体参与进来，这个合作更是前景可期。

架起桥梁，授业解惑

在浙大的学习已经进行了六个月，大山修习了河口学、近海动力过程、海洋信息处理等多门课程。他坦言自己的研究方向还没有确定好，目前继续在他感兴趣的海洋工程领域进行文献的阅读和整理，在知识海洋中徜徉并努力找到自己有兴趣的研究方向与项目。接着，在这个方向学深、学透，成为一名更加具有实力的科研人员。

古人云，"学高为师，身正为范"，知识会在传播与分享中拥有更大的价值和意义，这也是大山一直以来坚信并打算践行的。在浙大的研究生学习将持续三到四年，学习结束后，大山打算回到自己的国家，在以前的学校继续任职。

这里的他，如海绵般孜孜不倦吸收着先进知识技术；未来的他，会学以致用，在大学校园里继续以老师的身份活跃着，让知识在尼日利亚的土地上传播得更远更广。他相信，自己在有了浙大的学习经历之后，可以更好地授业解惑，让自己的学生也能够了解到中国的先进海洋研究成果。同时也会依托着大学的环境，继续科研，将自己的所学应用到更加实际的方向。

大山参加第三届中非海洋科技论坛
Samuel in the 3rd Sino-African Forum on Marine Science and Technology

大山是学校水上俱乐部成员
Samuel being a member of aquatic club of Ocean College

采访人：陆理宁

采访日期：2018年3月

Lifetime Learning

Six months ago, Samuel Ukpong Okon was an academic lecturer at Akwa Ibom State University in Nigeria. In as short as half a year, he is now a postgraduate student of the Ocean College, Zhejiang University, majoring in ocean engineering. From a teacher to a student, Samuel tirelessly pursues more advanced and cutting-edge knowledge and hopes to take it back home in the near future, in order to bridge China and Nigeria. Undoubtedly, this bridge of knowledge does not only support the advanced technology exchanges, but also gives hope for the future ocean prospects of the two countries.

Exploring High-tech in the laboratory

What is the experience of viewing, via acoustic-optical instruments, the hydrothermal fluids and exotic creatures thousands of meters under the ocean? What would it be like to be an aquanaut in a sleek and advanced 200-meter tourist submersible? What do the rare creatures of the far polar region look like? All of these fascinating and mysterious questions make the oceanographers excited.

Samuel and other international students finally got the answers to these questions on a recent field trip supported by the Chinese Government Marine Scholarship. In Shanghai, they visited the University History Museum and Deep Sea Exploration Pavilion at Tongji University, Hadal Science and Technology Research Center of Shanghai Ocean University, Port Base of Tongji University, East China Sea Bridge and Yangshan Deep-water Port, and Polar Research Institute of China, etc. What an unforgettable trip to the blue ocean.

China's powerful marine technology and sophisticated deep-sea equipment have deeply impressed Samuel shortly after he got here. Such surprises happen every day in the Ocean Engineering laboratory of ZJU where he was soon to be working. In the laboratory of Professor He Zhiguo, a doctoral instructor of Zhejiang University's Ocean College, Samuel saw many cutting-edge measuring instruments. "The LISST, the super high-speed cameras, and the professional mooring equipments are all for the student use. This is a perfect scientific research utility for me!"

Besides the strong marine scientific research capacity, ZJU also has a friendly and

welcoming research atmosphere. As a newcomer, Samuel was not familiar with the University environment. However, the hospitable volunteers, the comfortable dormitory environment, the friendly and harmonious interpersonal relationship made him love his life at ZJU. He also reached out greatly in the past few months. He had been to Beijing and Shanghai. China's great diversity constantly fascinated him.

Searching the academic direction

Samuel is like a ship in the sea of knowledge, sailing against the current. Professor He Zhiguo is the captain guiding him forward. According to Samuel, Professor He is both a conscientious and considerate.

Before meeting Professor He, Samuel searched online out of curiosity and excitement and read a lot about his instructor from his webpage. Samuel found that Professor He is mainly engaged in computational hydrodynamics, sediment dynamics, offshore dynamic processes, marine engineering environments, storm surge disaster prevention and mitigation. Every of them interest him to do research for. "I am delighted to discover that the research direction of my professor and mine go very well. He has so many excellent research achievements and publications that it is my luck to be his student."

"After meeting with him, I find that he is indeed as knowledgeable and intelligent a scholar as I learnt about." A small incident made Samuel much touched by Professor He's considerateness. Since Samuel's research includes a lot of computation, a powerful computer is essential. Considering that it would be inconvenient for him to shop on his own as Samuel first came, Professor He got it ready for him ahead of time so that Samuel could join the group and keep up with the learning as soon as he arrived.

After joining Professor He's research group, Samuel found more and more of Professor He's patience and sense of responsibility towards his students both in life and in study. "Professor He is the first person to whom I would ask for help and advices whenever I have problems. I can always get a response timely whether through email and WeChat, or by going to his office directly." What impressed Samuel even more deeply was that He Zhiguo was always active in the WeChat group of his research team to communicate with students about his experience and achievements in research, and to show the forefront research results he saw or heard. Every bit of sharing contains the good intentions.

Furthermore, Samuel was also deeply impressed by Professor He's rigorous academic work, which was like an alarm urging him on all the time. Under the guidance and help of such a strict instructor, Samuel thought that he could become more engaged in scientific research and learning. He said, "My instructor pays close attention to our scientific research. Even in the winter vacations, he would ask us to report our research work periodically, reminding us to finish the new semester plans and expectations." Regular group meetings were also important. Students took turns to report and discuss the progresses of their research. This was both an opportunity and a challenge for Samuel. He recalled the scene of being in the group discussion for the first time, "I introduced myself at the meeting, and then stated my own research ideas. I think it was a very good opportunity to present myself!" Samuel said with a smile.

Keeping Africa in mind and seeking for a win-win cooperation

In the vigorous development of China's marine industry, Samuel sees a good opportunity for the bilateral cooperation and mutual benefits. The oceans are the common wealth of mankind. Samuel, who is from Nigeria, looks forward to working with the Chinese scientists to make positive contributions to understanding, exploring, and exploiting the oceans. Keeping Africa in his mind, he hopes to know more of China, seeking for a way to facilitate the cooperation between the two countries in the marine study. It is worth mentioning that his Chinese name Dashan was given to him by his Chinese teacher. The well-known Canadian scholar and TV talk-show actor Mark Rowswell named himself Dashan in Chinese. He is an iconic person in the cultural exchanges between China and Canada. Perhaps it also contains the teacher's expectation that Samuel will become a messenger between China and Nigeria in the future.

The sea level rise is one of the environmental challenges internationally. Since the 20th century, the global sea level has risen by 10 to 20 centimeters. Although it is a slow onset of the natural disaster, it has significant adverse environmental impacts in the recent years. Some low-lying coastal areas are flooded; meanwhile the intensity and frequency of stormy tides are increasing. Nigeria, Samuel's country, is also affected and threatened seriously. This caused the constant attention and concerns of Samuel. A doer as he is, he started the relevant research on sea level rise since 2015, when he studied the effects of the rising sea levels on Britain's coastal areas and gave an academic report in North Wales, UK.

Not long ago, the Third Sino-African Forum on Marine Science and Technology was held in Hangzhou, jointly organized by the Second Institute of Oceanography under Ministry of Natural Resources of China and Zhejiang University. As one of the representatives in the forum, Samuel presented a report on the impact of the rising sea levels on the coast of Nigeria. In his report, he described the vulnerability of the coastlines, listed the potential impacts of the sea level rise and proposed the coastal management measures. As a researcher in the field of ocean engineering, Samuel is deeply aware of the importance of the knowledge about marine environment and development to the country and people. This is also one of the reasons for his study at Zhejiang University. He said "ZJU is committed to the cutting-edge ocean research, driving the science innovation and technical progress of many related areas in China and in the world."

Actually, the marine cooperation between China and Nigeria has a long history. In 2012, China sent the ocean expedition ship called Ocean One to implement a joint inspection with Nigeria, opening a new page for China's cooperative investigation of marine science and technology in the economic zone of African countries. In recent years, the win-win cooperation between China and Nigeria in ocean and other areas is developing with a sound momentum. With the overseas students like Samuel, the collaboration is more promising.

Bridging the gap to share the knowledge

It's been six months since Samuel came to ZJU. He has studied many courses, such as the Estuary, Offshore Dynamic Process, and Marine Information Processing among others. He told us frankly that he is still uncertain about his research direction, and that he is reading and collating the literature in the field of ocean engineering, trying to bridge his gap in this field so as to research deeply and thoroughly in this direction, and hopefully to become a more influential researcher.

As an ancient saying goes, "those with profound knowledge can be learned from, while those with nobility can be learned after." Knowledge is more valuable and meaningful in the sharing and spreading. Samuel believes in it and plans to practice. He plans to return to his own country and resume teaching in his former university after his three and a half years of postgraduate study at ZJU.

Right now, Samuel assiduously absorbs the advanced knowledge and technology like a sponge; in the future, he will apply his knowledge to his teaching in Nigeria, making it known to more Nigerians. He believes that after learning at Zhejiang University, he will be able to teach better, having his students understand China's advanced marine research.. At the same time, he will continue his research in the university, applying what he has learned more practically.

励志求学路，难忘浙大情

逆流而上，抱志以行

　　来到浙江大学海洋学院之前，汉森已经在自己的家乡谋得教职了，并且，他还是个"网络红人"：他在社交平台上向大家分享求学的经验、生涯规划的指导意见，拥有众多"粉丝"，甚至登上过巴基斯坦当地的采访节目，为报纸撰写励志文章。他从事着这样的工作：帮助年轻的孩子们实现自己的人生目标，培养他们坚忍不拔的品质。当被称为"励志演说家"的汉森说到自己的求学经历时，确实有许多故事可讲。

　　出生在巴基斯坦的乡村，生活对汉森来说并不轻松，他在贫困的家庭环境中长大，而在2002年，12岁的他更是经受了失去父亲的哀痛。为继续家里的生活、为亲人们分忧而承担的责任，经济上的巨大压力，顿时压在汉森稚嫩的双肩。普通的少年也许无法想象，正如玩具与美食进入他们的梦一样，书本与黑板的影像是怎样进入汉森的梦里的。无助包围周身之时，他险些放弃了继续接受教育的梦想。但是，在小汉森心里，知识与教育一直是他最珍贵的梦，像未经开垦的森林中出现的火光，他相信自己的梦不该结束，就算承受再多辛苦，他也想坚持下去。

　　怎么坚持呢？面对不得不直视的学费问题，汉森感到无力，幸运的是，他的中学老师在看了他的期末成绩后告诉他："你不该放弃学业。"并为他提供了足以继续接受教育的资金帮助。这无疑是天降甘霖，而得到了这样的信任与支持的汉森也没有辜负老师的期望，在2006年和2008年的升学考试中都得到了A等的好成绩。在他即将进入工程学院的时候，经济上的拮据还是阻断了他的求学之路，他不得不在一年内停止了学业。

2009年，巴基斯坦政府推行的奖学金政策给了他机会，他便开始准备这个项目的考试。这是他唯一的继续他的求学之路的希望。为此，汉森每天不顾辛劳地去离家60公里的免费考试准备培训班参加训练。凭着一股韧劲，汉森获得了全额奖学金并顺利读完了自己的本科与研究生，在陆地电磁通信、电子工程等领域掌握了基础知识。

如果将这些经历比作铺垫的话，真正对未来汉森人生道路产生决定性影响的，还要属浙江大学的一纸录取通知书。中国，浙江大学，海洋学院，当这三个崭新的词蹦入汉森的脑海时，汉森的人生新篇章真正开启了。为什么是中国？中国政府海洋奖学金是一个契机，它给来自巴基斯坦的汉森更大更高的探索平台，而中国能给予汉森的教育也是他梦寐以求的——他深感巴基斯坦对海洋研究的局限性，也意识到巴基斯坦在海洋领域的教育是非常欠缺的。同时，汉森对中国和中国文化一直抱有好感。在巴基斯坦，中巴友谊早已深入人心，中国像兄弟一样对待这个邻邦，也争取着双方的合作交流、共同进步。在中国留学的巴基斯坦朋友们也和汉森分享了留学经历，让汉森对中国的留学生活很是向往。汉森很喜欢中国古代思想家、哲学家老子的"千里之行，始于足下"这句话，他觉得这与他的学习态度非常吻合，道家思想等中国古代哲学思想对

他有着独特的吸引力，学习中国文化，体会中国特色，也是汉森来中国求学的一大

汉森竞选留学生班长并当选
Hassnain running for the monitor of 2017 international students

原因。而有机会在中国顶尖学府、推动高等教育事业改革发展重要一员的浙江大学读书，更让汉森觉得是无与伦比的幸运。他的家人们也全力支持他的留学之旅。于是，汉森收拾行囊，再次出发，踏上了中国的大地，来到了宁静迷人的浙江大学舟山校区。

汉森就读的专业为海洋信息工程，他的主要研究方向为水下电磁通信。选择这个研究方向，是汉森与博士生导师徐敬讨论的结果。在巴基斯坦时，汉森已对陆地电磁通信有了一定研究，因而转向水下电磁通信的研究时过渡困难相对较小。在提交申请材料时他的想法也得到了导师的认可。同时，徐敬导师带领的课题组主要研究方向是水下无线光通信，也需要开展水下电磁通信的相关研究以适应不同的水下信道环境。二者在学术研究和工程应用上有互补性，更利于海洋信息技术的发展。目前，汉森正在与课题组其他几位中国学生一起开发水下电磁通信样机，并于2018年暑假在舟山海域进行海试。

为了让汉森更好地适应中国的学习模式和专业培养，徐敬导师制定了详细的课题组管理制度，每周组织一次组会，与留学生们探讨课题研究进度、学习适应情况等。汉森也被徐敬导师鼓励着担任组会的主持人，锻炼自己的组织能力。同时，徐敬导师在课下会与汉森探讨学术问题，帮助汉森制定未来研究规划，也会要求他提交周报，汇报学习情况。徐敬导师希望，汉森以及其他留学生能积极融入海洋学院的大家庭，导师与学生互相帮助，齐心协力，把海洋信息相关研究做强做好，争取在部分技术指标上达到世界领先水平。

探索中国，乐在交流

汉森有个有趣的中文名字：哈哈。朋友们叫他哈哈，老师们也叫他哈哈。汉森非常喜欢这个名字，不仅朗朗上口、意义积极，也拉近了他与他人的距离。当大家喊他一声"哈哈"时，交流似乎也因此变得轻松愉快起来。汉森本就是个乐于分享、乐于交流的人，到了中国更是要放开眼界，好好"说一说"。

2017年11月，在上海举办了中国政府海洋奖学金第三次交流项目，浙江大学海洋学院参加了此次的游学活动。作为2017年获得中国政府海洋奖学金的留学生代表，汉森负责了开幕式的演讲。他的演讲主题围绕着浙江大学的国际化工作的方式方法和海洋研究两个方向展开。每每回想起这段经历，汉森都怀着幸福的荣誉感和崇高的敬意，因为对他来说，能有机会代表浙江大学表达观点，是对他能力提升有建设性影响的一次尝试。同时，在此次交流活动中，初来中国的汉森也结交了不少留学生朋友，他们一起参观上海，一起讨论学习生活，创造了美好的回忆。

汉森加入了海洋学院的留学生交流群，在那里，大家不仅可以交流学习生活上的体验，还组织了各种活动，丰富课余生活。比如汉森体验了国际乐器交流会，参加了学生社团，每逢节日，大家也会聚在一起。除了留学生，汉森也积极和中国学生交流，在食堂就餐时，他会与中国同学聊天，结交朋友，还会使用微信与朋友们联系。当然，他也用微信和远在故乡巴基斯坦的家人们联系，进行视频通话，使空间上的距离感远远缩短。

除了微信，为了在中国更方便地生活，汉森自己学会使用了网上购物软件并多次网购。他也下载了汉语词典，用电子词典自学汉语，而且，他还学会了

汉森（右1）在同济大学与同学们交流并发言
Hassnain (right 1st) exchanging ideas and
giving a speech in Tongji University

汉森在羽毛球比赛中获得混双第一名和男单第三名
Hassnain in the badminton competition

汉森（左4）与队友参加足球比赛
Hassnain (left 4th) in the football competition

使用手机支付。他对这些中国的应用软件非常满意。

为了将自己的交流经历"方法化"以便为他人提供帮助，汉森总结了他结交朋友的"套路"：多参加新生活动；勇敢地踏出第一步；参加社团、体育活动、聚会。

与人交流之外，汉森还与中国的风景名胜好好交流了一番。在中国的大半年里，汉森游览过北京、青岛、武汉等多个城市。游览的过程，也是和中国对话的过程。汉森看到了与故乡不同的人与景：北方城市的大气，南方城市的秀丽，沿海地区的开放，内陆地区的敦厚。无论是天安门还是长江岸，一切都深深吸引着汉森。不过，尽管大城市车水马龙、繁华热闹，汉森还是喜欢像舟山这样的海岛。在舟山，有浪拍海岸的悠闲，也有群山环抱的静谧，空气清新，民风淳朴，适合安下心来好好进行研究。

执着教育，终身所托

受到儿时经历的影响，汉森一直非常珍惜和重视教育。而当他实现自己的求学梦时，他的目光投向了更多在故乡像他一样渴望知识的孩子，投向了巴基斯坦仍有空白的教育事业。对于巴基斯坦乃至全世界，水下电磁通信这个领域属于科学研究的前沿，未来还有无限可能等待着学者们的探索。师者，传道者也，汉森就想成为一个传道者，把自己在浙江大学海洋学院学到的知识带回国内，发展教育事业，用自己坚持不懈的求学品质感染激励更多学生，培养未来人才。

在浙大的求学路是汉森人生的惊喜，也是他的幸运。惊喜和幸运都属于坚持奋斗的人，这是对汉森最好的奖励。自他收到这个"奖励"以来，他从没有忘记巴基斯坦的孩子们需要指导，没有忘记海洋研究领域留下的空白，没有忘记自己走过的长长道路——回头便是星夜下千卷的苦读灯影，前望便是建设祖国的一片光明。

采访人：张明珉

采访日期：2018年3月

汉森（第1排右）带浙大法学院学生游览舟山南洞艺谷
Hassnain (front right) guiding the international students from Guanghua
Law School, ZJU to visit Nandongyigu, Zhoushan

Unforgettable Zhejiang University

My dream drives me go upstream

Before coming to the Ocean College of Zhejiang University, Hassnain was teaching in his home country. He was also a star on the internet. He shared his academic experiences on the social media, giving advices. He had so many fans that he was invited to write for the local TV programs and for the local newspapers. His job was to help the young children fulfill their goals of life and make them persistent. When Hassnain, known as the encouraging speaker, talks about his own study experiences, he indeed has too much to say.

Born in the countryside of Pakistan, life was not easy for Hassnain. He grew up in a poor family. In 2002, at the age of 12, he suffered from losing his father. A huge economic pressure fell on the shoulders of the young man. It was hard to imagine for the ordinary teenagers how much Hassnain dreamed about the books and the blackboard in the way they dreamed about toys and food. Hassnain was about to give up his pursuit for study in those darkest days. However, education was his only dream. It was like a fire in the unknown forest, lighting up his path despite of the hardships.

But it was difficult. Hassnain felt hopeless in the face of the expensive tuition fees. Fortunately, after knowing his final grades, his middle school teacher told him, "You shouldn't give up." The teacher also sponsored him to continue his education. With such trust and support, Hassnain lived up to the expectations of the teacher. He scored A in the entrance examinations both in 2006 and 2008. When he was about to study in the College of Engineering, he was hurdled by the financial difficulties again. He had to quit after only one year.

In 2009, ICT R&D Scholarship supplied by the government of Pakistan gave him an opportunity to continue his education. He started to prepare for this scholarship test. As it was the only hope to continue his study, Hassnain travelled 60 kilometers everyday to attend free training classes. His efforts were paid off by winning the full scholarship for both his undergraduate and graduate studies. He learnt some fundamentals about electrical engineering and electromagnetic wave communication.

It was the admission letter from Zhejiang University that made the virtual change to

Hassnain's life. Ocean College, Zhejiang University, and China, seeing these three new words, Hassnain knew a new chapter of his life was to be unfolded. Why China? The Chinese Government Marine Scholarship is a wonderful opportunity for Hassnain to pursue his academic dream in a prestigious institute. On the one hand, he dreamed of Chinese education as he realized that ocean research and education in Pakistan was quite limited. On the other hand, Hassnain loves China and Chinese culture. In Pakistan, the friendship between the two countries is deeply rooted in people's hearts. China always treats this neighboring country like a brother and seeks for cooperation and exchanges in order to make progresses together. Hassnain's Pakistani friends studying in different Chinese universities shared their study experiences with him inspiring him to choose China for his further studies. Hassnain likes a well-known ancient Chinese saying of the great Taoism philosopher Lao-Tsi "A journey of a thousand miles begins with a single step." He thinks it is just how his study is like. The ancient wisdom has a unique attraction to him. Learning the Chinese culture and the Chinese characters was the main purpose for his coming. He felt so lucky being able to study at Zhejiang University, one of China's top universities in the frontier of China's higher education reform and development. It boosted Hassnain's confidence to study in China. Hassnain's family supported his decision as much as they could. Now, here he is—at the quiet and beautiful Zhoushan Campus of Zhejiang University.

Hassnain majors in the marine information science and engineering. His research is underwater electromagnetic waves communication. Choosing this research direction is the result of his discussions with his PhD instructor Professor Xu Jing. Hassnain had done some research in the electromagnetic communication on the land when he was in Pakistan. It would not be too difficult for him to shift into the underwater electromagnetic communication so that his application was accepted by Professor Xu. Meanwhile, the main research direction of Professor Xu's research group was underwater wireless optical communication. Underwater electromagnetic communication is also needed to adapt their research to different underwater communication environments. The two ways of communication complement each other and benefit the research. Currently, Hassnain is developing underwater electromagnetic communication prototypes with several other Chinese students and will try it out in the Zhoushan bay in the summer.

Professor Xu Jing set up a set of regulatory rules for the students. That helps Hassnain better adapt to the learning and training. On the weekly group meetings, the international students were invited to join the group discussions. Hassnain was highly encouraged by

Professor Xu Jing to serve as the moderator of the group. At the same time, Professor Xu Jing would discuss with Hassnain on various questions, help him make research plans, and ask him to submit weekly reports. Professor Xu Jing hopes that Hassnain as well as the other international students can become part of the Ocean College to make concerted efforts with the faculty and students on the marine information research and strive for a leading position in the world.

Love China and love the exchange

Hassnain has an interesting Chinese name: Haha (The Chinese word for laughing). His teachers and friends call him Haha. Hassnain likes this interesting name. When people call him by this word of a laughing sound, they seem to be closer to him. That way, the communication seems to be easy. Hassnain loves communicating with others to make new contacts.

In November 2017, the third Chinese government marine scholarship exchange program was held in Shanghai. The Ocean College students attended the program. Hassnain made a speech on the opening ceremony on behalf of the international students who came on the Chinese government marine scholarship in 2017. He introduced the internationalization and the marine research at Zhejiang University. He was so proud of the experience that he took it as an honor. Talking about this speech, he is extremely happy and full of esteem. He thinks that it has significantly improved his capacity. During this exchange program, Hassnain made a lot of good friends from different universities, with whom he visited different places in Shanghai and had an unforgettable time.

Hassnain has joined the international students' WeChat group. People share their study and life online and organize various events to enrich their extra-curricular life. With the group, Hassnain went to an international musical instrument conference. In holidays, the group would hold parties to celebrate.

Haissnain loves hanging out with the Chinese students. He would try to talk with the Chinese students and make friends with them in all possible occasions, whether in the cafeteria or on the playground. He learnt to use WeChat talking with his friends and making video calls back home.

Hassnain has also learnt to shop online via Taobao, and purchased different things online. This saves his time and makes his life easier. He is very pleased with such Chinese applications like Alipay and QQ. He has downloaded Baidu Translator and Pleco Chinese dictionary in order to learn Chinese.

Hassnain is always positive. He never fears to take the first step to make new friends. To help others make friends as easily, he summarized a list of the tricks of making new friends: actively participate in the school events, cultural festivals, trips, and parties; participate in the events for the new students; be the first to talk to others; join the student society; play sports; go to the gatherings…

Besides making so many friends, Hassnain has visited a bunch of scenic spots and beautiful cities. In the last six months, Hassnain has been to Shanghai, Beijing, Qingdao, Wuhan and Hangzhou. He has met with people from different areas and he appreciated the hospitality and love of this nation. He loves the generosity of the northern cities, the beauty of the southern cities, the openness of the coastal areas and the honesty of the inland areas. Whether Tiananmen or the Yangtze River, everything is charming to Hassnain. He loves the busy life and prosperity in the big cities, he also likes the beautiful islands like Zhoushan, where the blue mountains, fresh air, and honest folks create a peaceful place for a slow-paced friendly life and for the more focused research.

I'll teach in my whole life

Hassnain has always cherished and valued education due to his childhood experiences. As he has realized his dream, he hopes to bring opportunities to the children in his hometown, who are eager to learn as much as he does. As the underwater electromagnetic communication is a forefront technology with infinite possibilities, Hassnain aims to become a teacher when he goes back to Pakistan, so as to inspire more students.

Studying at Zhejiang University is a wonderful surprise to Hassnain as well as a blessing and forfune for him. As good luck only falls on those who strive for it, this luck is a reward for his constant efforts in his life. Ever since he has received this reward, he has never forgotten the Pakistani children who need his guidance, nor has he forgotten the unknown fields of ocean studies in Pakistan. He could never forget the harshness he has been through for his dreams. Looking back, he could see his profile of reading in the lamplight at the starry nights; looking forward, he expects a bright future for his country.

追梦赤子心

卡姆兰的南沙之旅
Kamran's trip to the beach of the South China Sea, Zhoushan

"上有天堂，下有苏杭。"——两年前，卡姆兰从在浙江大学玉泉校区就读的朋友口中听到了这样一个美好的杭州。朋友兴奋地与他分享了在浙大进行的有关机器人科学研究的经历，这深深地吸引了喜爱机器人的卡姆兰。从充满自然气息的巴基斯坦到钟灵毓秀的中国，从一个只是对机器人感兴趣的学生到成为第一支在OI中国水下机器人大赛中获奖的在华留学生团队队长，卡姆兰在浙江大学实现了一个个"不可能"，将所爱化为现实。

你好，浙大

申请硕士期间，卡姆兰就了解到浙江大学是中国的顶尖学府，科研实力雄厚，在他攻读的海洋工程和水下技术专业领域上更是有着极高水准。再加上朋友的推荐，他毫不犹豫地将浙江大学列为自己最心仪的学校。凭借本科优异的成绩，他进入了宋宏副教授负责的海洋光电与自动控制实验室，并在宋老师的推荐下获得了"浙江大学奖学金（A类）"，如愿开始了在浙江大学的生活。

这是卡姆兰第一次来到中国，全然陌生的环境对他来说既是挑战，更是机遇。直至飞机抵达杭州，他才有了新生活即将开始的实感。依依不舍地与杭州的朋友分别，初到舟山的他不会说中文，有着诸多的不适应，但一年半的时间让他越来越庆幸自己能来到浙大，来到舟山，来到海洋学院。无论是普陀岛的梵音涛浪、寺塔崖刻，抑或是岱山的石壁残照、鱼山蜃楼，都让他渐渐爱上了这个海滨城市。更重要的是，这里有着丰富的资源，这里有着优异的老师，这里能让他从事热爱的科学研究，这里能让他实现所爱所想。

而这样的转变离不开导师宋宏的支持。在卡姆兰进入实验室之初，宋老师考虑到留学生语言不通，若从事硬件研究，在购买零部件时将遇到诸多不便，便安排他进行软件方向的图像识别研究。但卡姆兰的心中始终有一个做机器人的梦。两个月过去了，卡姆兰一边完成手头的实验研究，一边自学了水下机器人的相关知识，最终向宋宏老师提出了转换研究方向的想法。在那段日子里，宋老师时常能看见卡姆兰在实验室的角落里安静地捧着书钻研。"他是一个很用功、喜欢自学、很有钻研精神的学生。"宋老师如此评价卡姆兰。这样一个认真好学又有想法的学生打动了宋老师，尽管实验室的主攻方向不是水下机器人的本体制作，他仍然全力支持卡姆兰做自己想做的研究。虽然宋老师平日因海洋局的工作十分忙碌，但他仍会抽出时间，细心地给卡姆兰上交的每一份报告做好批注，尽力解决卡姆兰在研究中遇到的问题，给予了他许多很有帮助的建议。

实验室也渐渐成了卡姆兰课后最爱去的地方，在那里，他徜徉于领域里最新、最顶尖的学术论文和报告，不断学习前沿创新新兴技术，与实验室的同事们相处得也越来越融洽。卡姆兰购买了零部件要报销发票，同事们都愿意热心地帮这个不会中文的巴基斯坦小伙子跑流程，而卡姆兰的开朗与好学也感染了他们。每当同事们在实验室里聊卡姆兰的研究时，一旦他们用中文提到"卡姆兰"，他总是会开心地插一句："什么？什么？"温馨欢快的实验室氛围、良好融洽的师生关系以及得天独厚的学术

卡姆兰（右）与导师在实验室第一次见面合影
Kamran (right) meeting his supervisor in the lab for the first time

环境化解了卡姆兰初来乍到的彷徨与不适，让他以更坚定的决心向着自己的目标前进。

你好，机器人

2017年，卡姆兰的机器人研究逐渐步入正轨，在宋老师的指导下，他和另外两位留学生参加了由中国海洋学会、国家海洋技术中心与励展博览集团联合主办的2017 OI中国水下机器人大赛，研发用于水下目标自动探索的智能机器人。作为唯一一支在华留学生参赛队，他们凭借自主设计研发的"海洋行走者水下机器人"获得了大赛三等奖。

天津水下机器人大赛中卡姆兰（前排左）在检查机器人
Kamran (front left) checking the robot in the competition in Tianjin

在短短三个月的紧张备赛期里，卡姆兰和两个同伴根据比赛日程倒计时，夜以继日地泡在实验室里。在着手准备比赛前，宋宏老师就向他强调：先想明白目标，再去实现，做出与现有水下机器人不同的作品才是关键。这对卡姆兰来说是一个重要的启示，也是一个很大的挑战，但在宋老师的悉心指导下，一个个困难得以解决。卡姆兰团队受到水下动物螳螂虾能用眼睛中超过5种颜色的受体在水下识别颜色的启发，希望让自己的机器人通过不同的色调和饱和度来识别不同颜色。有了这个目标，他们展开了一轮轮研究，通过图像传感器将信号送到控制器，而控制器通过权衡比例来识别颜色和形状。自信与坚持让卡姆兰直面问题、不断创新，实现了研究上的个个突破。

作为组长，卡姆兰在兼顾研发机器人的同时，还担任着领导者的角色，为组内成员分配任务，紧跟进度，这对他来说亦是一种锻炼。一个人在三个月里创造出梦想中的机器人很艰难，但值得庆幸的是，队友和导师始终支持与陪伴着卡姆兰。学校提供了先进的试验场地，老师为团队解决了项目经费，实验室的同学帮忙购买试验器材，浙大的老师和同学支撑着卡姆兰将梦想变成了现实，让他的"海洋行走者"最终遨游于辽阔的大海。

卡姆兰在中国水下机器人大赛中获奖照片
Kamran receiving an award in the robot competition, China

卡姆兰（左1）获得IEEEP主席和巴
基斯坦Mehran大学校长颁发的奖项
Kamran (left 1st) being rewarded
by the presidents of IEEEP and
Mehran University, Pakistan

对卡姆兰来说，这次比赛检验了他的学习和研究能力，给了他获得发展的机会，对帮助他进一步深化相关领域的研究有着重要的意义。在比赛中，他不仅接触到了许多领域内的前沿知识，还结识了新的朋友，赛后更受到了一些中国公司的青睐，表达了与他合作展开相关研究的意愿。2018年，卡姆兰还将自己在这次中国比赛中取得的水下机器人研究成果带回了巴基斯坦参加比赛，在由巴基斯坦电子电气工程机构（IEEEP）举办的第三十三届巴基斯坦学生研讨会中一举斩获了第一名的好成绩。当卡姆兰兴奋又骄傲地拿出奖状时，不难看出他对水下机器人研究的喜爱与自豪。本科时的兴趣成了今日的成就，他很高兴能与浙大共享这份源于热爱和坚持的荣誉。

你好，未来

如今已是卡姆兰来到中国的第二个年头。两年间，他去过上海，到过杭州，走过天津和青岛，但只有舟山这座波涛铺展开的城市深深地扎在了他的心里。初到舟山时语言不通、生活不便的情景似乎还在眼前，而如今的卡姆兰已会说一点中文，学会了使用中文的地图软件和网上购物软件。他还笑着说道："我去年还留下来过了中国新年，学校带我们吃了许多传统美食，留下了许多美好的回忆。我现在越来越觉得自己像个中国人了。"令卡姆兰印象深刻的是，每当他迷路了，向遇到的当地市民问路时，他们虽然不太会说英语，但总是会想尽办法给他指路。中国人民的善良、诚实和友好也让卡姆兰越来越想学好中文，走近这个美丽的国家，走近那些独特的文化，走近这群可爱的人。

在学业上，卡姆兰也适应了与原先大学不一样的教学方式，在文献分析、项目实践上都有了新的见解。他也在不断完善着自己制作的水下机器人，立志在发现水下濒危物种上有所贡献。而卡姆兰现阶段正全身心投入撰写相关研究的总结报告，期待能在期刊上发表。在宋宏老师的指导下，卡姆兰将在下一阶段的研究中更注重水下机器人的载体作用，把时下热门的人工智能融合到水下机器人的机器视觉研发上，从而对目标进行更精准的判断和识别，达到自动分类的效果。

一年半的时间看似短暂，却已经让卡姆兰和浙大建立起了深厚的感情。卡姆兰常常说，浙里的生活为他的未来打开了一扇扇新的大门，带他通往他所向往的知识世界，帮助他适应了国际化的环境。谈及未来，对水下技术着迷的卡姆兰想一直学习下去，他打算在拿到硕士学位后，继续攻读博士学位。毕业后，他想加入一家从事水下技术研发的企业或相关的国际组织，继续开展他热爱的水下机器人科研攻关。

这个将研究水下机器人当作最大爱好的巴基斯坦小伙子毫不犹豫地说，来到浙大是他做过的最好选择。浙大是深入学习、做好科研的理想园地，浙大是一个值得被爱的地方。在这里，他实现了梦想，而梦想也照进了他所期望的未来。

采访人：徐奕宁

采访日期：2018年3月

I Love My Country

"Suzhou and Hangzhou are Paradise on earth." Two years ago, Kamran heard about Hangzhou from a friend of his, who was studying at Yuquan campus of Zhejiang University. His friend told him about his research on robots at Zhejiang University with such an excitement that Kamran, also a robot lover, was deeply attracted. Through effort, Kamran was enrolled in Zhejiang University. In the university, he built up the first international student team of OI and became the leader in chief, leading his team to attend the China Underwater Robot Competition. The team won the third prize. Kamran made the impossible possible time after time during his stay at ZJU.

Hello, ZJU

While applying for the master's program, Kamran learnt that Zhejiang University is one of the top universities in China, with strong scientific background. His major—marine engineering and underwater technology is an advanced discipline in the university. Affected by his friend's exciting story-telling, he applied for Zhejiang University without any hesitation. Thanks to his excellent undergraduate performance, he was granted the Zhejiang University Scholarship (Class A) and joined Marine Optical Sensing Laboratory run by Dr. Song Hong.

This is Kamran's first trip to China. The brand-new environment is full of challenges and opportunities. When his airplane landed in Hangzhou, he realized his new life started since then. When he first arrived in Zhoushan, he had a lot of difficulties in his daily life since he couldn't speak any Chinese. However, one and a half years later, when he looked back, he said it was a right decision that he came to Zhoushan campus. His love for the city grew in time, not only for its beautiful landscape but also for its resources. The teachers he met in Zhoushan are also very helpful. This is the perfect place to make his dream come true.

Dr. Song Hong, Kamran's instructor has helped Kamran a lot. At the beginning, Dr. Song was worried that Kamran would have difficulties purchasing parts due to his language barrier if he was arranged to deal with hardware, so that he had Kamran study image recognition algorithm instead. However, Kamran always had a robot dream. Two months later, Kamran studied underwater robots in his spare time on top of the assigned experiments. After that, he asked Dr. Song for a transfer to the research on the underwater robots. Noticing that Kamran usually read quietly in the corner of the lab, Dr. Song agreed to his request, "He is a very hard-working and self-motivated student. I know he will do well in his research." said Dr. Song. His diligence and sincerity impressed Dr. Song so deeply that he supported Kamran firmly despite that the underwater robots were not his focus. Although Dr. Song is very busy with his job at the Bureau of Ocean and Fisheries, he read through every of Kamran's reports carefully and tried his best to help solve the problems Kamran encountered in the study.

The lab became Kamran's favorite place, where he could stay and study the latest and the most advanced underwater technology and innovations. Gradually, he got along well with the other students in the lab. When Kamran was in need, they were willing to help. When Kamran bought some parts that need reimbursement, they helped him with the complicated administrative procedures. And they were also motivated by Kamran's diligence. When the students mentioned "Kamran" in Chinese, Kamran would pull his neck "What is it? What is it about me?" Thanks to the friendly relationship in the lab, Kamran had overcome all the discomfort and inconvenience and became more determined towards his goals.

Hello, robot

In 2017, Kamran's underwater robot research was on track. Guided by Dr. Song, he and two international students participated in the 2017 OI China Underwater Robot Competition organized by China Ocean Society, National Ocean Technology Center and Reed Exhibitions. They developed an artificial-intelligence robot that can be used for underwater searching and rescuing. As the only international student team, they won the third prize in the competition with the Ocean Strider Underwater Hybrid Robot, which they developed independently.

In the 3-month's preparation, Kamran and his two teammates worked day and night in the lab. Dr. Song emphasized to him from the very beginning "Set your goal first, and then go for it. The key is to make a robot that is distinguishable from the existing ones." For Kamran, this was an inspiration as well as a challenge. With Dr. Song's help, they tackled the difficulties one after another. Inspired by the mantis shrimps, which can recognize colors in underwater environment with the 5 or more objects of different colors, the team built their robot with the ability to recognize different colors through different hues and saturations. With the target, they made many times of experiments, sending signals to the controller via the image sensors to have the controller distinguish colors and shapes by comparing their appropriations. With confidence and persistence, they overcame difficulties, made breakthroughs, and finally succeeded with the innovation.

As the group leader, Kamran had to give assignments and follow up with the progresses. It was difficult to create a dream robot in three months, but thankfully, his teammates and mentors always backed him up. The college also provided the advanced test sites and funding for the team. The Chinese students in the lab helped them to purchase the components. With such help, Kamran turned his dream into reality, and their Ocean Strider was able to walk on the floor of the ocean.

For Kamran, the competition proving his capability of learning and doing research, provided him with the opportunities for his further development. It was of great importance for his further research in the related fields. During the competition, he got to know the cutting-edge technology in the field and made some new friends of the same interests. After the competition, some Chinese companies expressed their willingness to cooperate with him in the research. This year, Kamran brought his Strider to the 33rd Pakistan Student Seminar organized by the Institution of Electrical & Electronics Engineering Pakistan (IEEEP). He won the first prize! He was so excited and proud of it. His love for the underwater robots was evident all the time. When his dream from his college years came true, he wanted to share the glory and honor with Zhejiang University.

Hello, future

It is the second year of Kamran's stay in China. In the past two years, he has been to Ningbo, Shanghai, Hangzhou, Tianjin and Qingdao, etc., but Zhoushan has been home to him. "I still remember how difficult it was when I first arrived in Zhoushan, not knowing the language," Kamran said. Now, Kamran can speak some Chinese. He has also learned to use the mobile phone APPs, such as the Baidu map and the online shopping. He told us pleasantly, "I spent my Chinese New Year here last year. The university brought us traditional Chinese food and gave us a Red Packet, leaving me a lot of wonderful memories. I enjoyed it. I feel myself more like a Chinese now." What impressed Kamran most is the kindness of the local people. When he got lost and asked for directions, they would try their best to help him out, although they didn't speak English. The kindness, honesty, and friendliness of the Chinese people make Kamran more interested in learning Chinese to get closer to this beautiful country, its unique culture, and its lovely people.

Academically, Kamran has adjusted himself to the different teaching methods in China. He has also developed new insights into the literature analysis and project practice. His underwater robot is also under constant improvement. Now, Kamran focuses on writing reports, summarizing his research in hope of publishing. Taking Dr. Song's advice, Kamran will pay more attention to the applications of his underwater robot in his next phase of study. He will apply the popular artificial-intelligence methods to the vision development of the underwater robots, so as to better distinguish the objects and classify them automatically.

One-and-a half years seem short, but Kamran has been strongly bonded to Zhejiang University. Kamran often says that his life in Zhejiang University opens a new door to his future, leading him to the academic land that he dreams of, and adapting him to the international world. Fascinated by the underwater technology, he hopes to continue studying for his doctorate degree after his graduation. After that, he may go to work for a company or an international organization to continue his research on the underwater robots which he loves so much.

This passionate Pakistani young man thinks that coming to Zhejiang University is the best choice he has ever made. Zhejiang University is an ideal place for studying and doing research. It deserves all your love for it. It is at this place where he realized his dream and starts to dream of his future.

在中国遇见新的自己

多元文化塑造了他

罗伊是个巴基斯坦和加拿大的混血儿。因为父亲在巴基斯坦和加拿大两国经商，罗伊在卡拉奇和多伦多两个城市长大。卡拉奇作为巴基斯坦重要的港口城市，融汇了现代和古代文明，可见古城窄巷，亦可见高雅的现代建筑；而加拿大的多伦多作为著名的国际大都市，有着多元的族裔特色。罗伊就是在这样丰富包容的文化环境中长大的，而这也塑造了现在的他。

在巴基斯坦取得计算机工程专业学位后，罗伊来到迪拜开始了工作。当他作为网络工程师在一家公司工作的时候，他一直在留心观察着公司与公司、地区与地区、国与国之间的各种竞争，当他把眼界放到全球视野时，他发现中国在科技方面取得了非凡的成就，并仍在飞速发展之中。作为一个敢于挑战、充满干劲的年轻人，为了使自己拥有竞争力，更为了寻找更多机会与可能，罗伊决定出国留学。

罗伊选择了中国，是因为他在工作中看到了中国科技的力量，也了解中国是一个有着悠久历史和灿烂文明的国家，深知它正在高速发展，并已经是世界经济强国。他相信中国是一个充满机会的国度，也希望自己能有机会到中国留学，了解更多中国的文化。

没有梦想，何必远方。当罗伊下定决心要来中国留学后，他开始了行动。

有些人认为，出国留学便意味着一笔巨大的开销，而罗伊在了解到中国的奖学金项目后，消除了这个误解，积极地进行了申请。2016年2月，罗伊果断地辞去了在迪拜的工作，来到加拿大帮助父亲工作。经过五个月的等待，在2016年7月，他终于收到了来自他的"梦之乡"中国的邮件，被浙江大学录取。他永远不会忘了那时的激动和惊喜，对他来说，能获得浙江大学A类奖学金，有机会在这样的大学学习，成为顶尖教授的学生，提升自己的技能和经验，实在是令人难以置信！当他的父母知道儿子将去中国顶尖高校攻读硕士学位时，也非常满意欣喜，表示全力的支持。

来到中国，罗伊很快适应了新环境。浙江大学海洋学院所在的舟山在他眼里是一个可爱的小城。这座小城为他提供了世界级的购物、娱乐环境，很多全球连锁的西餐厅他都能找到。同时，舟山也是一个美丽的城市，这里人们安居乐业，风景秀美，空气清新，有着一种恬静的气质，为罗伊提供了一个良好的生活学习环境。在饮食上，习惯尝试各地风味的他爱上了中国菜，他为自己常常能吃到美食而开心。罗伊乐于认识新朋友，他在课堂与课余时间里结交了许多中国朋友，他们一起进行各种户内外活动，看电影、做烧烤，也去旅游，到海边吹吹海风，聊聊天。

在浙江大学，罗伊的生活充满惊喜，有许多值得期待的事物。他认为，教育不仅存在于课堂之上，也存在于社会的实践活动中。他很在意一个安全和舒适的环境，他强调要促进自我学习的能力。在浙江大学，全年都有各种各样的学生活动，浙大提供了许多室内和户外运动项目及场地，包括篮球、乒乓球、羽毛球、桌球，体育馆、游泳池和足球场，罗伊会使用这些场地锻炼身体。同时，作为留学生，罗伊也被欢迎加入各种中国传统节日的活动和聚会中，比如中国的春节、元宵节、端午节等，还有新年晚会。在罗伊的校园生活之外，他已经游历了中国的许多城市：上海、杭州、天津、广州、义乌、宁波、青岛等。他以不断探索的热情观察着每个城市。他发现，每一个城市都有属于自己的美丽。若要问起他最喜欢的城市，回答便是：上海。罗伊觉得他最想居住在上海，因为上海作为一个国际化大都市，有着开放包容的文化气质，沿海人民灵活变通的处事风格也和他本人的做事风格非常契合。面对一些不同的生活方式和文化习惯，罗伊表示，他知道在某些方面，事情当然会有所不同，如生活习惯、文化风俗。但在中国留学，需要有求同存异的态度。这是最重要的。他也知道在中国的城市居住，会出现一些由于与自己长大的城市风格不同而产生的矛盾冲突，但他认为这些都是学习的机会，只要抱着包容学习的心态，这将会让他更加了解中国的文化，也更加珍惜文化的多样性。

中国教育培养了他

在罗伊的浙大留学生活中，有一个人起了非常重要的作用，那就是他的导师徐敬教授。罗伊主要的研究方向是水下光通信，这与他之前主修的计算机工程有着联系和承接性，同时他还参加了徐敬老师带领的一个课题。谈到自己的导师，罗伊感到非常幸运，因为徐敬老师不仅在研究项目上给予了他专业的帮助，同时也非常通情达理、关心学生。考虑到罗伊的性格和学习习惯，徐敬老师给予了罗伊"自由的实验室时间"，也就是说，罗伊可以在确保每周总工作时长合格的前提下灵活安排自己的科研时间。同时，徐敬老师也常和罗伊讨论研究进度，在每周一次的组会上，他会鼓励罗伊主持，锻炼他的组织能力，也使他对课题组的研究有更深入的了解。当罗伊感到迷惑时，徐敬老师会耐心指

罗伊（右1）和导师徐敬以及实验室同事游览舟山东沙滩
Roy (right 1st) visiting Zhoushan east beach with his tutor Xu Jing and his lab colleagues

导他的研究工作，并鼓励他通过脚踏实地的努力战胜暂时的困难。在师生配合努力下，罗伊已顺利完成了几项实验任务，并作为第一作者发表了一篇EI国际会议论文。

在实验室工作时，罗伊感觉自己置身于一个大家庭。作为一个团队，在导师徐敬的带领下，课题组的成员们互相帮助，一起努力取得更多的突破。罗伊与小组成员相处得非常融洽，他的同伴们评价他是一个积极开朗的男孩，有很强的适应新环境的能力；他充满了好奇心，有很强的动手能力，善于使用计算机软件，并非常乐意帮助他人，是做实验的好搭档。中国同学的友谊帮助使罗伊很快适应了中国的学习生活，也让他得到了动力，变得比以前更加独立和灵活。作为团队的一员，他慢慢学会把自己放在一个集体中行动，找到适合自己的位置，发挥自己的特长和作用。

对罗伊而言，在浙江大学留学的时间里，他在学业上做出的最大的改变，便是勇敢地走出了自己的"舒适区"，学会在一个有竞争亦有合作的教育环境中训练自己的思维，了解并着手研究新的领域。

罗伊（左3）在天津参加水下机器人大赛和队友合影
Roy (left 3rd) in the underwater robot competition in Tianjin with his team

罗伊（右1）与同学们在湖边做实验
Roy (right 1st) doing experiments with his classmates on the lake

生活是一场美丽的冒险

在中国留学的时间给了罗伊思考职业规划的机会。在来到浙江大学海洋学院进行系统学习前，罗伊就对自己的未来有所打算，抱有在中国工作的想法，而如今的专业学习更让罗伊坚定了未来要在中国创造一番事业的决心。

罗伊的父亲是一名商人，而罗伊并没有选择子承父业，这也得到了父亲的支持。罗伊说，父亲不只有着自己的生意，而且还是一名土木工程师。父亲重视儿子的教育，非常支持罗伊来中国继续学习的决定，并且鼓励他专注于学业，承担起自己的责任，为自己的梦想奋斗。

罗伊未来的职业规划与在浙江大学的专业学习有着很大的关联性。罗伊计划于2019年毕业后从事与信息通信相关的行业，也许创办自己的公司，也许申请进入华为这样的中国通信科技公司。

生活对于罗伊来说，"每天都是一次冒险"。为了更好地了解中国，罗伊喜欢用自己学会的普通话和中国人交流，也许是出租车司机，也许是商店的店主，也许是浙大校园里一个投来微笑的同学。他也加入了留学生组办的学生会，和来自各国的留学生们交流旅行经历，丰富自己的见闻。罗伊睁着大大的眼睛看着这个奇妙的国度，在这里，文化的碰撞、融合奏出了崭新的乐章，有数不清的东西供他学习思考。对他而言，每天都是新的，因为每天都能接触到新的东西。学习中国的语言、中国的文化和研究自己专业的知识一样，都令罗伊感到愉快和兴奋。

来到中国是这个"冒险家"的一个美丽的决定，而在浙江大学的留学生活带给了罗伊很多收获。罗伊意识到自己多元化的追求在此地得以实现，他将会继续学习，继续创造难忘而独特的浙大记忆、中国记忆。

采访人：张明珉

采访日期：2018年3月

Meeting the New Roy in China

Grew up in a diversified culture

Roy has heritages of Pakistani and Canadian. He grew up in two cities, Karachi and Toronto, since his father does business in Pakistan and Canada. As an important port city in Pakistan, Karachi has integrated the modern and ancient civilizations, narrow lanes and elegant modern buildings. While as a famous international metropolis, Toronto of Canada has its multi-ethnic characteristics. Roy was brought up in such a rich and inclusive culture.

After earning a degree in computer engineering in Pakistan, Roy moved to Dubai for his first job. Working as a network engineer for a company, he kept an eye on the competitions between companies, regions and countries. As he expanded his horizon to the whole world, he found that China has made remarkable achievements in science and technology and is developing rapidly. As a young man full of energy and ready for challenging status quo, Roy decided to study abroad to improve his competitiveness and to seek for more opportunities and possibilities.

Roy chose China because in his work he came to see the strength of China's science and technology. He also knew that China is a country with a long history and splendid civilization, and that it is developing rapidly and has become a world economic power. He believed that China is a country of opportunities and hoped he himself could have the opportunity to study in China and learn more about the country's culture.

Without a dream, there is no need to travel far. Once Roy made up his mind to study in China, he took actions. Some people think studying abroad means a large sum of money. But after learning about the scholarship program offered by the Chinese government, he cleared up the misunderstanding and applied eagerly. In February 2016, Roy decisively quit his job in Dubai and went back to Canada to work for his father. After five months of waiting, in July 2016, he finally received an email from his dreamland—China, and was admitted to Zhejiang University (ZJU). He would never forget the joy and surprise at that moment. For him, it was incredible that he could get the Class A scholarship of ZJU, be given the opportunity to go to such a prestigious university and study under top rate professors to improve his skills and experiences. When his parents learned that their son was to study in one of China's top universities for his master's degree, they were overjoyed and gave him their full support.

In China, Roy was quick to adapt to his new environment. Zhoushan, where the Ocean College of ZJU is located, is a lovely place in his eyes. It supplies him the world-class shopping, entertainment and many of the global chain restaurants serving western food. At the same time, Zhoushan is also a beautiful city, where people live and work contently. Its beautiful landscape and fresh air make it a quiet and pleasant living and learning environment. For a man who loves to try different local flavors, he has fallen in love with Chinese food, and is happy that he can often try local delicacies. Roy loves to meet new friends. He has made a lot of Chinese friends in his spare time after school. They have had a variety of indoor and outdoor activities together, such as watching movies, barbecuing, travelling, and enjoying the sea breeze and the chats on the beach.

At ZJU, Roy's life is full of surprises. There are many things to look forward to. He believes that education exists not only in the classroom, but also in social practices, and a safe and comfortable environment is important for self-learning. On the campus, a variety of student activities are organized throughout the year. Available also is a rich selection of indoor and outdoor sports, including basketball, ping pong, badminton, and billiards, as well as gymnasium, swimming pool, and football fields, where he often goes for a work-out . At the same time, as a foreign student, Roy has been invited to all kinds of Chinese festival celebrations, such as the Spring Festival, Lantern's Day, Dragon Boat Festival, and so on.

Beyond Roy's campus life, he has traveled to many cities in China: Shanghai, Hangzhou, Tianjin, Guangzhou, Yiwu, Ningbo, Qingdao and others. He observes them with an unceasing zeal for exploration. He finds that every city is beautiful in its own way. If you ask him about his favorite city, the answer is: Shanghai. Roy believes he would want to live in Shanghai, because as an international metropolis, Shanghai has an open and inclusive culture, and the flexible and adaptive working style of the coastal people also fits well with his style. Regarding different lifestyles and cultural practices, Roy says he knows that in some ways things will of course be different, such as living habits and cultural customs. But studying in China, it is important to adopt the attitude of seeking common ground while putting differences aside. He also understands that living in a Chinese city, one might encounter clashes or conflicts with the life style of where he grew up. But he believes that all these are learning opportunities. As long as he takes an inclusive, receptive attitude, such opportunities will lead to better understanding about the Chinese culture and a deeper appreciation of the diversity of cultures.

Fostered by the Chinese education

One person who plays a very important role in Roy's student life at ZJU is his instructor, Professor Xu Jing. Roy's main research direction is the underwater optical communication, which is related to and consistent with his previous training in computer engineering. He also participates in a project led by Professor Xu. Talking about his instructor, Roy feels extremely lucky, for Professor Xu has not only provided him with valuable professional help in his research, but is also very reasonable with and caring for the students. Given Roy's personality and learning habits, Xu allocates Roy with a free laboratory time policy, which means he can arrange his research time flexibly as long as he ensures that his total work hours are up to par. Meanwhile, the professor often spends time discussing the research progresses with Roy. At the weekly group meeting, he would encourage Roy to host the session to train his organizational ability and improve his understanding of the research details of the whole group. When Roy becomes confused, Xu would patiently offer guidance and encourage him to overcome the temporary difficulties through his down-to-earth efforts. With the help of Professor Xu and the fellow students, Roy has successfully completed several experimental tasks and published a paper in EI international conference as the first author.

Working in the lab, Roy feels like being in a big family. As a team, under the leadership of their instructor Xu Jing, all members of the research group assist each other and work together to strive for more breakthroughs. Roy gets along very well with his team. His peers describe him as a positive and cheerful boy with strong ability to adapt to the new environment. Full of curiosity and known for strong hands-on ability, Roy is good at using computer software, willing to help others and is a good partner to do experiments. The friendship with his Chinese schoolmates helps Roy acclimatize to his student life in China pretty soon, and motivates him to become more independent and flexible than before. As a part of the team, he has gradually learned to put himself in a collective action, find his position, and play his own strengths and roles.

For Roy, the biggest change in him during his study in ZJU is that he has bravely stepped out of his "comfort zone", learned to train his mind in a competitive and cooperative education environment and is ever ready for new frontiers.

Life is a beautiful adventure

The time spent studying in China gives Roy a chance to think about his career planning. Before Roy came to the Ocean College of ZJU for a systematic training, he had a plan for his future with the idea of working in China. And the professional study here has strengthened his determination to do something big in China in the future.

Roy has decided not to follow the footsteps of his businessman father, whose support for his choice being a good reason. Roy said his father not only runs his business, but is also a civil engineer. The father values his son's education, supports Roy's decision to continue studying in China, and encourages him to focus on his discipline, shoulder his responsibilities and pursue his dreams.

Roy's future career planning is closely related to his study in ZJU. He hopes to work in the ICT industry after graduating in 2019, perhaps starting his own company, or applying to join a Chinese communication technology company like Huawei.

Life for Roy is "an adventure every day". To get to know China better, Roy likes communicating in the Mandarin whenever possible with Chinese people, be it a taxi driver, a shop owner or a smiling fellow student in ZJU. He also has joined the student union organized by overseas students, and traveled with overseas students from various countries to enrich his knowledge and broaden his mind. Roy opens his eyes wide at this wonderful country, where the collision and fusion of cultures play a brand new movement, and where countless things await for him to learn and to think about. Every day is new to him because he is exposed to new things. For him, learning Chinese language and culture is just as enjoyable and exciting as studying his major discipline.

It is a beautiful decision for this adventurous young man to come to China. Studying abroad in ZJU has benefited Roy immensely. He realizes that his diversified pursuit is coming to fruition here. He will continue to learn and create the unforgettable and unique memories of ZJU and of China.

到大海中寻药去

方框眼镜后一双深邃的眼睛，浓浓的一字眉，闭着的双唇，纳吉布的外貌给人一种沉静的感觉。他是来自巴基斯坦的浙江大学海洋学院2014级博士研究生。在浙江大学海洋学院的这几年，舟山温柔恬静的气质、浙大大气严谨的科研氛围、中国和谐善良的文化传统，都在潜移默化地塑造着纳吉布，也帮助他成为一个更优秀的人。

在来到浙江大学海洋学院之前，纳吉布是一名生物科学领域的教师，也在制药行业担任过医疗销售人员。基于这些工作经验，纳吉布产生了对使用天然产品，特别是海洋生物制药研究的兴趣，并希望通过接受继续教育，深入研究有关海洋自然资源在制药领域的应用。但在巴基斯坦，对海洋资源以及海洋资源在制药方面的应用的研究并不多，纳吉布能学习到的知识非常有限。于是，纳吉布把眼光放到了海外，他希望能在有先进实验室和教育水平发达的学校接受系统的教育，而浙江大学正是能满足他这个需求的大学。怀着对更高教育的渴望，纳吉布参加了中国高校研究生项目，申请攻读浙江大学的博士学位，并最终获得中国政府奖学金的全额资助。

纳吉布的专业为海洋药物学。在刚进入浙江大学海洋学院时，纳吉布仅是怀着对这个专业的兴趣与对未来研究学习的期待，但他缺乏在实验室学习的经验，也没有足够的研究经历，一切都从零开始。更为纳吉布的学习增添难度的是语言上的障碍。尽管接受了语言培训，纳吉布对中文的掌握情况却并不好，如果说日常生活中的交流还能勉强应付，可专业文献资料上的中文对这个来自巴基斯坦的留学生来说难度实在太大。面对这样的情况，纳吉布的博士生导师吴斌教授给予了他最大的帮助和支持。

吴斌教授表示，他在纳吉布以及其他留学生身上花了比中国学生更多的精力与时间。在做实验时，吴斌教授会手把手亲自指导纳吉布，教他正确使用操作软件、仪器设备，得出更为准确的实验数据。而对于纳吉布的汉语短板，吴斌教授在日常的课程学习中对他进行了语言上的帮助，为他解释有难度的专业名词和概念，并引导他在面对中文文献时有意识地进行阅读训练，掌握文本的含义。在每周进行的组会中，吴斌教授会让纳吉布作一个报告，汇报自己的研究进度，展示对吴斌教授布置的文献资料的阅读成果。对于纳吉布每周的报告，吴斌教授给予了很高的重视并提出自己的指导意见。吴斌教授说，每周和纳吉布的讨论时长都有好几个小时。同时，他还鼓励纳吉布和其他学生阅读专业领域内的优秀文献，定期进行文献总结，提出自己的想法和解读。

经过吴斌教授的指导，纳吉布慢慢"入了门"，对海洋药物学产生了浓厚兴趣，他表示这种兴趣将会延续一生，同时，随着实验室学习经验的增长以及知识的不断丰富，纳吉布在学术研究上取得了突破。2017年，纳吉布作为第一作者发表了一篇ESI高被引论文。

"已经有一篇好论文了，但是我希望纳吉布还是要多加把劲。"吴斌教授对纳吉布的进步感到欣慰，但也对他提出了更高的要求和更多的期待。吴斌教授表示，他将继续督促纳吉布在学业上努力，利用好中国宝贵的教育资源，多出些科研成果，这对纳吉布将来的发展大有帮助。毕业后纳吉布打算回到巴基斯坦，在浙大的学习经验必将成为他实现梦想、开拓美好未来的基础，基于这样的考虑，吴斌教授一直在帮助纳吉布，指导他在学术上打下坚实的基础。

对于导师如此的关照，纳吉布内心充满了感激之情。而纳吉布与吴斌教授的师生情不止存在于学习上的交流，也存在于平时交往的默契中。

在生活上，吴斌教授对纳吉布非常关心，他对纳吉布的宗教信仰（伊斯兰教）给予了最大的尊重。在饮食方面，初到中国时，纳吉布对中餐风味很不适应，但学校为他提供了自己烹饪的空间，他可以在那儿制作清真食品，他也会参加学院或导师组织的聚餐，体会中国多元包容的饮食文化。在家庭方面，初到中国时，纳吉布的思乡情绪比较强，这也影响了纳吉布对新环境的适应。吴斌教授理解纳吉布的心情，也为他提供了适应的时间。他体谅纳吉布一年回巴基斯坦一次不易，便给他延长假期时间，让纳吉布得以有更充足的时间和家人们相聚，度过美好的家庭生活，好好休息。在平时，纳吉布用视频的方式和家人们联系，由于时差的影响，纳吉布也许会与家人们聊天到深夜，吴斌教授注意到了这一点，允许纳吉布在第二天早上晚一些来到实验室，这些理解让纳吉布非常感动，吴斌教授在他眼里是一个良师益友，他也带着感激和信任的心情面对这样一位好老师。

谈到未来，纳吉布表示，毕业后他将继续从事海洋药物学的研究工作，并努力助力发展祖国巴基斯坦的制药行业。吴斌教授指出，海洋药物学有着很大的发展潜力，目前对于海洋领域的研究相对滞后，更需要投入科研力量推动，它的进步将对人类健康做出巨大的贡献。这是超越国界的，不仅仅关乎"名声"，更关乎"民生"。而在赞许纳吉布、对他充满期望的同时，吴斌教授对纳吉布提出了回国后谋得一个教职的建议。提出这个建议，既是基于他对纳吉布的观察和了解——因为纳吉布的性格沉稳，做事踏实，性格上非常适合教师

纳吉布（左3）在浙江大学海洋学院与课题组同事合影
Najeeb (left 3rd) with other team members in Ocean College, ZJU

这个职业；也是吴斌教授作为导师的希望。吴老师给予了纳吉布在职业规划方面的实际指导，在巴基斯坦，教师这个职业受人尊敬，同时纳吉布也可以得到较高的薪水，供养他的家庭。纳吉布慢慢理解了老师的用心，也决心回国后在继续研究海洋药物的同时能成为一名老师，为教育事业做出贡献。

纳吉布在中国的旅游照
Najeeb on the trips in China

在学习生活之外，纳吉布也在体味着中国这个充满魅力的国家的风土人情。在与中国人交流的过程中，他发现中国人非常真诚、勤奋和乐于助人。他形容中国人"有合作精神"，在平时的交往中，他们总能积极交流，相互合作。在和中国学生一起学习的过程中，他感受到中国人对待自己的工作的热情与投入。在他的中国之行中，杭州和上海给他留下了很深的印象。他见过秀美的西子湖，也见过满载历史的黄浦江，这两座城市，一个是温柔的"人间天堂"，一个是大气的"东方巴黎"，纳吉布都很喜欢。在游览中国的城市时，纳吉布发现，中国的城市都很整洁，人们对环境保护非常重视，如倡导垃圾分类，在进行城市区位设计时工业区总位于盛行风的下风向。他也表示，这样努力减少污染的尝试值得巴基斯坦学习。更吸引纳吉布的是，在中国英语的普及度已经很高，语言上的沟壑正在慢慢被填平，这将为他和向他一样的外国人提供便利，可以促进文化上的交流，在掌握语言的基础下，纳吉布能更清楚地了解到中国的美丽。

由于专注学业，纳吉布并没有参加太多校内外的活动，这与他的自我定位有着密切的关系。正应了吴斌教授的期望，他希望能在中国的留学过程中尽可能多地学到专业知识。已经过了不惑之年的纳吉布，明白自己的责任和担当，他希望自己能在攻读博士学位的阶段不负时光，学有所成地回国。在浙江大学海洋学院的学习生涯的开始，也是他人生第二篇章的序曲，在这里，他重新做回学生，接受理想的教育，为今后的职业生涯奠定基础。在其个人时间线上，这将是浓墨重彩的一个印记，在这里，他认定了海洋药物学的研究方向，决心在这个领域有所建树，最重要的是，能为巴基斯坦的自然科学研究、制药业和教育事业做出自身所能创造的最大价值。尽管他也有懈怠的时候——吴斌教授说，如果为他的表现评分，品行和学习规范都是优，勤奋度只能打良好，但纳吉布也在慢慢进步，向中国学生的勤奋学习。

一切的现在都孕育着未来，未来的一切都生长于它的昨天。毕业的时间悄然接近，纳吉布的"浙里"生活也有期限。但知识是没有尽头的，回忆是没有尽头的，一切将被这位巴基斯坦的学生记住，并在将来的医药实践上、三尺讲台上以另一种方式展现出来。在浙大学习，到大海寻药去！希望，并且为它奋斗，纳吉布的梦想，就在他自己的肩上。

采访人：张明珉

采访日期：2018年3月

Looking for Medicines in the Ocean

A pair of deep-set eyes behind the frame glasses, thick eyebrows, tight lips, and a stern expression—it is the look of a young man named Najeeb，a grade 2014 PhD candidate from Pakistan at Ocean College of Zhejiang University（ZJU）. In the past few years at the university, the quiet temperament of Zhoushan, the rigorous research atmosphere of the campus and the generous and harmonious cultural tradition of China have subtly shaped his words and deeds, making him a even more outstanding man.

Before coming to the Ocean College of ZJU, Najeeb was a teacher of biological science and also worked once as a pharmaceutical salesperson. Based on his work experiences, Najeeb developed an interest in the application of natural products, especially in the research of marine biopharma. It was his hope to further study the application of marine natural resources in the pharmaceutical area through re-education. But in Pakistan, due to a lack of research and application in the field, the knowledge that could be learned was extremely limited. So Najeeb set his sights overseas. He hoped to receive some systematic training in a school with advanced laboratories and high educational attainment. And ZJU was exactly the kind of university that met his demand. With a burning desire for a higher education, Najib took part in the Chinese university graduate program, applying for a PhD at ZJU. He was eventually granted a full Chinese government scholarship.

The major that Najeeb chose is marine pharmacology. Upon his arrival at the Ocean College of ZJU, he only had some interest in this field and expectations for his future research. However, as he lacked prior experiences in either the laboratory work or the research, he had to start everything from the very beginning. What was more, the language barriers placed additional difficulty on him. Although Najeeb had been given linguistic training, his mastery of Chinese was not adequate. He could get by with oral communication in daily life, but the level of Chinese in professional literature proved too much for the young Pakistani. Fortunately, Professor Wu Bin, Najeeb's doctoral instructor, stepped in to offer him timely help and maximum assistance.

Professor Wu believes he has spent more time and energy on Najeeb and other foreign students than on their Chinese peers. Here is an example, in order to help Najeeb obtain more accurate experimental data, Professor Wu guided him personally on how to use the lab instruments and operate the software. As for his problematic Chinese, Professor Wu added a language course to his daily study, explaining difficult scientific terms and concepts and guiding him to train consciously in reading Chinese literature and comprehending their texts. In the weekly team report, Professor Wu would arrange Najeeb to describe his experiment progress to demonstrate what he had learned from the literature readings assigned by the professor. To Najeeb's weekly presentation, Wu paid keen attention and always offered his own suggestions and comments. Each week, the professor spent hours in discussions with Najeeb. Moreover, he encouraged Najeeb and other students to read some outstanding literature in their field of expertise, make regular reading summaries, and present their own ideas and interpretations.

Thanks to the painstaking tutorship of Professor Wu, Najeeb slowly got started and has developed a strong interest in marine pharmacology, an interest, he believes, will last a lifetime. At the same time, with the growth of his laboratory experiences and expertise, he scored a breakthrough in academic research. In 2017, Najeeb published an ESI Highly Cited Paper as the first author.

"Even with a good paper published, I still hope that Najeeb could work harder." Professor Wu is gratified by Najeeb's progress but also places higher demands on and held more expectations from him. Wu promises to continue to urge Najeeb to intensify his academic efforts and make full use of China's precious educational resources to yield more research achievements. That would be of great help to Najeeb's future. Since the young man intends to return to Pakistan after graduation, the academic experience in ZJU will be a cornerstone for fulfilling his dreams and opening up a better future. With this in mind, the professor has been actively helping Najeeb and guiding him to build a solid academic foundation. The care and help from his tutor fills Najeeb with a strong sense of gratitude.

Their teacher-student friendship exists not only in academic communication, but also in daily life. Professor Wu shows full respect to Najeeb's religious belief (Islam). Najeeb was not used to Chinese food when he first arrived in China. So the University provided him with a separate cooking space, where he could prepare halal food. He also attends dinner parties organized by the School or his professor. Such occasions help him experience China's diverse and inclusive dietary culture. Najeeb suffered from homesickness in the early days, which once affected his adaptation to the new environment. Professor Wu saw the situation and left him ample time to acclimatize himself. The professor would extend his holiday time so he could have more time with his family during his annual trip home. Noticing that Najeeb likes to talk with his family via video calls which often last late into midnight due to time difference, Professor Wu would allow him to come to the lab a bit later in the following morning. Najeeb truly appreciates Professor Wu's special care and in his eyes, Wu is not only a teacher, but also a close friend worthy of his heartfelt gratitude and deep trust.

With regard to the future, Najeeb would like to continue to work on marine pharmacology after graduation and help develop the pharmaceutical industry in Pakistan. Professor Wu points out that marine pharmacology is blessed with enormous potential. Since the current study in the field is lagging behind, more research input is needed. But its progress would produce immense benefits to human health. The efforts transcend beyond the national boundaries. It's not just about the fame of the researchers, but also about people's livelihood. While appreciating his decision and holding expectations from him, Professor Wu nevertheless suggests that he first secures a teaching post after returning to Pakistan. The idea is based on Wu's observation and understanding of him. Because of Najeeb's calm and steady personality, being a teacher could be a suitable choice. It is also a career that Professor Wu, as his instructor, would hope him to pursue. The professor has supplied quite a bit of practical guidance in career planning. In Pakistan, teaching profession is well respected and well paid. So it would be easy for him to support his family. Najeeb has gradually come to see his professor's point and made up his mind to become a teacher to contribute to the cause of education while continuing his study in marine pharmacology after he returns to Pakistan.

Besides his study and daily life, Najeeb is also learning to appreciate the local conditions and customs of this charming country. He finds Chinese people very sincere, diligent and helpful. He describes them as "cooperative" and has no trouble in communicating actively and collaborating with them. While interacting with Chinese students, he keenly feels the Chinese people's enthusiasm for and devotion to their work.

Among the places he has traveled in China, Hangzhou and Shanghai have left a deep impression on him. He visited the charming West Lake and the Huangpu River, a witness of Shanghai's tumultuous past. Of the two cities, one features the exquisite "paradise on earth" and the other, the magnificent "Paris of the East". Both of them attract him strongly. What strikes him also is how clean and tidy all China's cities appear. People pay great attention to the environmental protection and have taken to waste sorting and positioning of industrial areas downwind. He believes that these attempts to reduce pollution should be followed in Pakistan. What's more appealing to Najeeb is the fact that so many people now speak English in China, and the language gap is slowly being filled out. This will provide convenience to and promote cultural communication for foreigners like him. With a good mastery of Chinese, Najib is now able to better appreciate the beauty of China.

Focusing solely on research, Najeeb stays out from most of the social activities either inside or outside the campus, a choice closely related to his self-positioning. As in response to Professor Wu's expectations, he hopes to learn as much professional knowledge as possible in China. Although already in his 40s, Najeeb is well aware of his responsibilities and commitments, and he hopes that he can maximize his time to work hard in his PhD program to reach his academic goal. His study career at the Ocean College of ZJU is also a prelude to the second chapter of his life. Here, he re-enters the school and receives the ideal education to lay the foundation for his future career. And this will be a milestone in the time line. He has already chosen his research direction of marine pharmacology, and made up his mind to achieve results in this field. And most importantly, it would allow him to make the utmost contribution to Pakistan's natural science research, pharmaceutical industry and education cause. It is true that there has been times when he kind of slacks off. As Professor Wu puts it, if his performance, conducts and studies are rated excellent, his diligence can only be rated good. But Najeeb is improving himself, albeit slowly, and learn to study as hard as his fellow Chinese students.

All at present is a preparation for the future, while everything in the future grows out of its past. As graduation is quietly approaching, Najeeb is down-counting his days at ZJU. But knowledge is infinite, so is memory. All are to stay in the mind of the Pakistani student and appear in different forms in his future medical practice and on the podium as a teacher. Study well at ZJU and look for medicines in the ocean! Keep hopes alive and fight for them! In pursuit of his life goals, Najeeb will find that his dreams are on his own shoulder!

萨迪克·以斯哈，一个研究石头的男孩

志在远方，扬帆起航

萨迪克·以斯哈，一个来自巴基斯坦小镇的男孩。在来中国之前，他是这样形容自己的家庭的，"中产阶级，家里的生活情况时好时坏，像坐过山车一样漂浮不定"。就在这样一个"漂浮不定"的家庭中，他做到了小镇上大部分人都做不到的事情，他在巴基斯坦开伯尔—普赫图赫瓦省北部的汉古镇完成初中和高中学习之后，选择了继续在白沙瓦大学（Peshawar University）深造，接受高等教育，并获得了理学学士（荣誉）、理学硕士和哲学硕士学位，成为一名优秀的大学生。

但以斯哈的求学梦远不止如此，获得世界一流大学的博士学位才是他长期以来的最终梦想。为了圆他的博士梦，他在家人的支持下义无反顾地选择申请攻读中国博士学位的项目。这对整个家庭而言是一个冒险的决定。这不仅意味着以斯哈从此要远离故乡和亲人，更意味着未知的挑战和不确定的生活。但幸运的是，他凭借自己出色的能力和优异的成绩收获了中国顶尖大学之一——浙江大学的录取通知书并攻读海洋地质学专业。

5个小时的飞机旅程让以斯哈开始觉得中国并

以斯哈在北京
Izhar in Beijing

不是一个很遥远的国度，从飞机下来本该感到陌生的他抬头第一眼看到的，便是他的巴基斯坦学长。在同乡的指引下，本以为会饱受语言沟通困扰的以斯哈感受到了杭州这个城市给予他的最大的善意，他几乎没有费什么力气就完成了报到、注册等一系列烦琐的入学手续。"中国人的热情和周到让我开始想去了解这个国家的文化，我想我是爱上了她。"以斯哈这样说道。

而真正让以斯哈感受到中华文化魅力的，是他在北京游玩的经历。在北京，以斯哈见到了紫禁城的华丽壮美，见识到了长城的雄浑壮阔，北京这座城市向他揭开了这个古老又神秘的国度的面纱，让以斯哈沉浸在这个陌生的国度浩瀚的文化海洋中。

浙里生活，浙里成长

在经过对各类项目的仔细比对后，以斯哈决定选择李春峰教授作为自己的导师，成了李春峰科研团队的一员。"我觉得这是我做过的最正确的决定之一。"以斯哈提道，"李春峰教授对待我们非常友好，他对待学术专业的态度和精神让我觉得跟着他可以学到真正的知识。"

就是在这样一名认真负责的导师的指引下，以斯哈开启了他在舟山的学术生涯。在舟山，以斯哈常常对着一块石头研究到深夜。海洋地质学的专业特性

以斯哈（左7）在浙江大学海洋学院与同学老师的合影
Izhar (left 7th) with his classmates and teachers at Ocean College, ZJU

让以斯哈开始痴迷于跟各种各样的石头打交道，有时甚至忘记了自己的休息时间，以至于他的导师李春峰经常性地提醒他："要多注意锻炼身体呀。"

但是李春峰导师不知道的是，以斯哈是一个十足的足球运动爱好者，早在巴基斯坦的时候，以斯哈就展现出了优秀的足球天赋。在科研之余，以斯哈经常约上三五好友，一起去体育场踢球为乐。不仅如此，以斯哈还多次从舟山来到位于杭州的紫金港校区，参加这里举办的各类足球比赛，通过足球这项运动更好地融入浙大这个大家庭。

同样，以斯哈也坦言浙大对他的帮助是他能够顺利完成科研的重要前提。和一般的只坐在实验室的工作不同，以斯哈的研究项目跨越了两个国家、四个地区。以斯哈的研究灵感源于巴基斯坦广阔的田野，在研究的初期，以斯哈经常跑去巴基斯坦进行实地考察。那是一个有着丘陵山脉的坚硬地带，陡峭的山

以斯哈（第3排左2）在浙江大学海洋学院与足球队的合影
Izhar (3rd row, left 2nd) with the football team at Ocean College, ZJU

以斯哈在巴基斯坦实地考察
Izhar doing the on-the-spot investigation in Pakistan

以斯哈在喜马拉雅山小山谷
Izhar at the valley of Himalaya

路、危险的河流，都给以斯哈的岩石采集工作带来了很大的障碍。以斯哈的岩石采集范围从巴基斯坦北部的Mansehra到Skardu。在如此大的范围内采样，让以斯哈不得不连续两天睡在喜马拉雅山脉的一个小山谷中。

而如何将这些样品运回中国同样是一个不小的挑战。这些石头通关需要一大笔费用，由于各个实验室的条件不同，这些岩石还需要被分装运输到武汉和廊坊两个实验室中。正是导师李春峰不停地帮助以斯哈在三地的实验室周转，并通过实验室的基金支持，才帮助以斯哈完成了这次跨国的研究项目。

而这仅仅是困难的开始，在分析研究过程中，以斯哈不止一次两天三夜不间断地工作以确保分析结果的准确。但庆幸的是，以斯哈不只是一个人在奋斗，在无数个外人眼中无比枯燥的重复研究过程中，他得到了武汉实验室潘博士的支持和陪伴，并在潘博士的帮助下顺利完成了课题研究。这也让以斯哈时

以斯哈（右）与武汉实验室潘博士合影
Izhar (right) with Dr. Pan in the lab, Wuhan

以斯哈实验室课题研究环境
Izhar's lab

常心怀感激。他经常说："我很感激李教授和潘博士的善良，他们对我无私的帮助让我顺利完成了我的课题，浙江大学真是一个学术研究的天堂。"

情谊未尽，来日方长

以斯哈与中国的情谊早已从浙大扎根，并开始不断发芽成长。以斯哈坦言，自从来到中国之后他就迷上了中国的饮食文化，尤其爱吃麻辣烫。"难过的时候就会去吃一顿麻辣烫，当舌尖感受到那一丝辣意伴随着面和菜的香味咽进肚子里时，就觉得不那么难过了。"以斯哈讲道。

留学的路总归是孤独的，以斯哈也是如此。他时常想念自己在巴基斯坦的父母和亲人，想起他们对自己的关怀和爱护。但庆幸的是，以斯哈碰到了研究团队里很有趣的一群人。这个团队中的留学生们在精神上总是互相扶持、互相鼓励，一起在这个相对陌生的国度里完成他们的科研梦想。虽然在团队合作过

程中不免争吵与拌嘴，但是这个团队带给以斯哈的，永远是家一样的温暖。

在来中国的这几年里，以斯哈曾担心过的最大的问题就是语言上的障碍。虽然他曾经在浙江大学紫金港校区学习过基础的中文，但是这些中文还不足以让他应付在中国的日常生活。以斯哈也曾努力学习过，但中华民族丰富的语言文化还是让他败下阵来。不过让以斯哈惊讶的是，他周围的人都可以用英语流利地和他进行交流，他几乎不费什么时间就能够很快地融入这个新的家庭，他还和李春峰导师成了很好的朋友。

以斯哈打算毕业后回到在巴基斯坦的父母身边多陪伴他们，并带着自己在浙江大学学到的知识在巴基斯坦找一份工作，或是继续从事一些科研上的工作。不管是选哪一条路，以斯哈都忘不掉自己在中国的这段无比难忘的经历，并梦想着有一天能带着父母和自己的家庭再次回到中国，让身边最亲爱的人也同样感受一下中华文化的魅力。

虽然以斯哈即将离开中国，但那些在舟山看到的风景、在武汉遇到的人们，都未曾离开过以斯哈的心中，哪怕半步。

采访人：刘俏言

采访日期：2018年3月

Sadiq Izhar, a Boy Who Studies Rocks

Setting Sail for the Distant Goal

Sadiq Izhar is a boy from a small Pakistani town. Before coming to China, he described his family condition as "middle class, but often with big ups and downs, like riding a roller coaster." With such a "drifting" family, he did what most people in his town were unable to do. After completing his junior and senior high school in Hangu, north of Khyber Pakhtunkhwa, Pakistan, he chose to continue his studies at the Peshawar University, where he received his degrees, Bachelor of Science (Hons), Master of Science, and Master of Philosophy, as an outstanding student.

But Izhar's dream was far from ending here. He had long dreamed for a PhD degree from a world-class university. With the support of his family, he resolutely went on to apply for a Chinese PhD program. For the entire family, this was a risky decision. It did not only mean that Izhar had to stay far from his hometown and family, but also had to face unpredictable challenges and uncertainties. Fortunately, thanks to his outstanding capability and academic records, he was admitted by Zhejiang University (ZJU)—one of the top universities in China—to study marine geology.

The five-hour plane journey made Izhar start to believe that China was not a very distant land after all. What came to his sight the moment he stepped on the strange land was a senior student from his own country. Under the guidance of his fellow countryman, Izhar, who had expected to suffer great communication difficulties due to the language barrier, actually met the greatest goodwill from the city of Hangzhou. He had virtually no trouble in completing a series of complicated enrollment procedures, such as check-in, registration and so on. "Chinese people's hospitality and thoughtfulness prompt me to seek an understanding of the culture of this country which I think I'm already in love with." Izhar says.

And what really allowed Izhar to feel the charm of the Chinese culture was his trip to Beijing. There, he saw the majestic Forbidden City and the magnificent Great Wall. The city of Beijing formally lifted the veil of this ancient and mysterious country, and Izhar found himself deeply immersed in the vast cultural ocean of this strange land.

Live and grow up at ZJU

After careful comparisons of different projects, Izhar decided to apply for the one under Professor Li Chunfeng's instruction. He became a member of the professor's research team. "I think this is one of the most correct decisions I have ever made." Izhar later said, "Professor Li is very friendly to us, and his attitude towards academic profession reassures me that from him I can learn true knowledge."

It was under the guidance of such an attentive and responsible instructor that Izhar started his academic career on Zhoushan campus. There, the young Pakistani often stays up late into midnight to scrutinize a piece of rock. The characteristics of marine geology fill Izhar with an obsession with stones. Sometimes he even forgoes his time for rests. Worried, Professor Li has to constantly remind him of "paying more attention to keeping fit".

But what the professor doesn't know is that Izhar is in fact a zealous soccer fan. As early as in Pakistan, he already showed his remarkable talent in sports. After the research hours, he often invites friends to the stadium to play soccer. Not only that, he also travels from Zhoushan to Zijingang campus many times for the soccer games. The games helped him better blending into the ZJU big family.

Similarly, in scientific research, Izhar also admits that the help from ZJU has been a vital prerequisite for him to complete his work load. Unlike a task limited to only laboratory work, Izhar's research project spans two countries and four regions. His research has been inspired by the vast fields of Pakistan. In the early years of the study, he often went to Pakistan for field trips. It was a hard terrain with mountains, precarious trails and dangerous rivers. They were considerable obstacles to Izhar's rock collection missions which covered a vast area from Mansehra to Skardu in northern Pakistan. Such extensive sample-collections forced him to spend nights in a small valley in the Inner Himalayas for two days in a row.

How to transport these samples back to China proved to be a big challenge. Going across the customs cost him a large sum of money. Due to the different conditions of each laboratory, the rocks also needed to be shipped separately to the other two laboratories in Wuhan and Langfang. It was Professor Li who constantly helped Izhar's commuting between the laboratories of the three places, and supported him with special lab fund with which Izhar was eventually able to complete this cross-border project.

And this was only the beginning of the difficulties. During the analysis process, Izhar had to, more than once, work non-stop for two days and three nights to ensure the accuracy of the analytical results. Fortunately, Izhar was not alone. In the process of those endless repetitive studies seen as extremely boring by countless outsiders, he was supported and accompanied by Wuhan laboratory's Dr. Pan, whose assistance was instrumental in the completion of the project and to whom Izhar always feels indebted. He often said, "I am grateful for the kindness of Professor Li and Dr. Pan. Their unselfish help allows me to complete my research, and ZJU is indeed a paradise for academic pursuit."

The ever growing and lasting tie

Izhar's tie with China has taken roots in ZJU and begun to grow. Since he came to China, he has been fascinated by the Chinese food. One of his favorite dishes is "spicy hot pot". "Whenever I feel low, I go and stuff myself with a large spicy hot meal. The moment I gulp down those delicious food I will instantly feel better." claims Izhar.

To study abroad is inevitably some lonely experience and it is the case with Izhar. He often misses his parents and relatives in Pakistan, and thinks of their care and love. But luckily, he has with him a group of interesting people in the research team. The international students in the team always give moral support and encouragement to each other to fulfill their research dream in this relatively unfamiliar country. Despite the occasional and probably unavoidable quarrels and bickering in the process of group work, the team brings to Izhar the comfort and warmth of a family.

In the past years of living in China, Izhar was worried about the language barriers, regarding it as the biggest problem in communication. Although he once received basic Chinese training on Zijin'gang Campus, such rudimentary level proves inadequate for him to cope with a daily student life in China. He tried hard to improve the situation, but had to back down in face of the nation's rich language culture. However, to his surprise, people around him can communicate with him fluently in English. Thus he was able to quickly integrate into this new family, and became very fast friends with Professor Li.

Izhar intends to live with his parents in Pakistan after graduation. With the knowledge he's learned at ZJU, he hopes to find a job or continue to do some research work at home. Either way, Izhar would not forget his unforgettable experience in China and dreams that one day he would return to China with his parents and his family, to let those closest to him experience the charm of the Chinese culture.

Although Izhar is about to leave China, the enchanting sights in Zhoushan and helpful people in Wuhan—he would never let them disappear from his memory, not even for a briefest moment.

在第二故乡扬帆起航

"作为留学生在浙江大学学习,是怎样一种体验?"

"一两句话很难说清,不过我从第一次来到中国,就爱上了舟山,爱上了浙里。"

小麦色的皮肤、干练的短发、明亮又炯炯有神的双眼,是邱凌留给笔者的第一印象。寥寥数语勾勒出他的中国情缘。紧接着,邱凌在浙里的故事伴随着他抑扬顿挫的流利英文娓娓道来,如同一幅精美的画卷,在笔者面前缓缓展开。邱凌是Aqeel Abbas的中文名。

邱凌在海洋科学大楼前的第一张照片
In front of the Marine Science Building—Qiu Ling's first picture at ZJU

我的第二故乡：从巴基斯坦到中国

邱凌来自巴基斯坦，是家里唯一出国留学的孩子，因此获得了全家的大力支持。来中国读书是他一直以来的梦想，终于在大学毕业之后得以实现。就这样，他漂洋过海来到一个陌生的国度，只为追求心中那份单纯的喜欢与理想。

"在刚来到中国的这段时间里，因为中文不够好，我还担心过如何与当地人交流、如何采购生活用品、怎样出行等。"不过从邱凌如今轻松的口吻中可以得知，当时的他完全是多虑了。"随着时间的推移，我和朋友们一起学会了使用淘宝、支付宝、微信和滴滴等软件，这些应用让一切变得如此简单，很好地帮助了留学生在中国的日常生活。在这里大部分超市都可以使用移动支付，而这些高新技术在我的故乡巴基斯坦都是没有的。最有意思的是，我居然在淘宝上买到了自己民族的食品！"通过邱凌绘声绘色的讲述，我们欣喜地得知他早已适应了在中国的生活，俨然一位"本地男孩"。而当被问起在中文尚未熟练的情况下如何使用淘宝时，邱凌露出了得意的笑容，向我分享起了他的心得："我一般会用英文输入我需要的东西，对检索出的商品图片进行对比，再结合价位决定买哪一件，其实特别方便。"

谈到在故乡巴基斯坦和在中国学习生活的最大不同，邱凌坦言道："在学术研究方面，浙江大学有很多专业领域的高科技仪器、浓厚的科研氛围以及更高的平台供我施展拳脚；在日常生活方面就如同我刚才所说，中国的网络实在太发达了，很多时候我都要忍不住向家乡的朋友们感慨。总的来说，中国让我感到：一切皆有可能。"

除了被学术与生活上的方方面面所吸引，邱凌同样对中国美景情有独钟，一山一水、一草一木他都想去亲自涉足。"趁学术研讨的机会我去过北京和杭州，但由于时间关系，没能亲身领略万里长城和西子湖畔，非常希望能再去一次。而我也利用周末和朋友游玩了舟山的很多地方，月亮湾、普陀山都是很美的。但要说我最喜欢舟山的一点，大概是在这里能看到大海吧，在我的家乡，看海几乎是不可能的。"说到这儿，我脑海中浮现出邱凌倚窗眺望的情景，目光所及之处不仅是深不可测的海域，更是同波涛一起熠熠闪光的理想。

　　对于邱凌来说，中国与巴基斯坦虽截然不同，但都是他深爱的地方。"我一直将中国视为我的第二故乡，她不是一个地方，而更像是一种情结。这便是我来到浙江大学读书最真实的感受。"邱凌深情款款地诉说着与中国结缘的一点一滴，而我仿佛看到了他眼神中散发出的憧憬与坚定。

邱凌（左1）游览杭州西湖雷峰塔
Qiu Ling (left 1st) at Leifeng Pagoda, the West Lake of Hangzhou

邱凌在舟山月亮湾
Qiu Ling at Moon Bay, Zhoushan

扬帆起航：梦想从浙里开始

因为邱凌现在导师的研究方向和他的兴趣非常一致，再加上浙江大学有更多研讨会和对外交流的机会，可以在很大程度上提升他的科研能力，于是，邱凌毅然决然选择了将"浙里"作为他梦想的起点。

"到浙江大学这样的顶尖大学学习是我一直以来的梦想，收到录取通知书的那一刻，我感到无与伦比的兴奋。"回忆起当时的情景，邱凌显得无比激动，仿佛时光倒回了故事开始的那一天。"想象一下，我第一次来到中国，便见到了来自世界各地的国际友人，有机会和他们一起在中国最好的大学之一学习，我该有多么幸运！"

而最令邱凌难以忘记的还是他来到浙江大学的第一天。据他所说，遇到大家的感觉就像在家里一样温馨。"那是我第一次和我的导师李春峰博士以及海洋地球物理与地球动力学课题小组的同学们见面，由于一些学术要求的原因，我比原定时间晚来了一个月，错过了冬季学期的课程。但是我的导师对我说：'这个学期你没上课，那么你应该去北京参加一个研讨会。'于是我和一个国际学生Akinrinade Opeyemi一起出席了在清华大学举办的斯坦福大学Amous Nur教授的学术报告会。"提起这段经历，邱凌语气中满是对导师的感谢，"那是一段非常难忘的经历和一个很好的学习平台，也让我对未来的科学研究产生了一些新想法，这都要归功于我的导师——李春峰老师。"

提起自己的得意门生邱凌，李老师脸上立马浮现出自豪的笑容。"邱凌作为留学生，有时候甚至比中国学生还要好学，整体感觉不浮躁，很安静，在学习的时候格外专注。"与此同时，李老师还表示对邱凌研究生阶段的学术成果抱有很大期望，他认为这无论是对巴基斯坦的海洋事业，还是对中巴两国的关系都大有裨益。

除了李老师的鼎力相助，来自同学的关爱也是邱凌进步道路上的基石。"在这里我认识了特别多同专业的中国朋友，当我有不会的问题时，总能第一时间找到解决方案。而最让我感觉如家般亲切的是，我在浙大遇见了来自本国的同胞——Mudaber、Farhan和以斯哈。来自巴基斯坦老乡的帮助最能温暖人心。"

当我开始自己的研究工作时，遇到了很多困难。但是我遇到了文爱，一个中国女孩。当我在研究中遇到问题时，她总会帮助我。她是我在中国遇到的很友善的人之一。希望她能取得很好的研究成果并顺利毕业。

邱凌在巴基斯坦的母语是乌尔都语，因此，英语和汉语对他来说都需要不断加强和练习。他目前主修海洋地质与地球物理学，具体科研领域是利用海底地震仪研究南海海盆的深部构造。而就算这一个连中国学生都认为有难度的专业，在邱凌眼里依然"学起来几乎没有遇到任何困难"。当笔者带着好奇向他取经时，他道出了迎难而上的法宝。"导师和中国同学都会在学业上帮助我，主动关心我，我有很多机会去向大家学习。在这样互帮互助的环境之中，我真的很难感觉到阻力与困难，也从来没抱怨过学业的辛苦。"

如果说邱凌的学术生涯是一艘蓄势待发的帆船，那么浙江大学便是梦开始的地方，故乡是他疲惫时停泊的港湾，而一路走来遇到的老师和同学就如同恰到好处的风，不断助他一臂之力。这正印证了那句"好风凭借力，助我上青云"。帆船即将起航，纵使需要乘风破浪、风雨兼程，依旧没有停下过航行的轨迹。

邱凌（左6）在进行徒步旅行之前与李春峰教授研究小组合影
Qiu Ling (left 6th) with Professor Li Chunfeng's team before a hiking

邱凌（右2）与来自缅甸曼德勒大学的两位教授访
问海洋学院期间合影
Qiu Ling (right 2nd) with two professors from
Mandalay University, Myanmar while visiting
Ocean College

情深似海：情谊比山水更绵长

"我的中文名字'邱凌'的灵感就来自于中国山水。这个像天堂般的地方
拥有一切你能想象到的自然美景，山川，湖泊，岛屿……还有来自祖国的朋友
和友好的中国人给我以故乡的感觉，他们就像山一样，给了我帮助和依靠。"

在繁忙的课业生活以外去世界各地走走停停是邱凌的一大爱好。旅途中他
总能遇到有趣的人和事，或渺小，或宏大。在这伟大与平凡的交织中不断丰富
着他对世界的理解。来到中国已有半年之久，邱凌表示并不怎么想家，因为他
在中国的很多城市都有留学生朋友，假期就会去他们所在的城市旅游，在领略
自然山水之美的同时体会友情的美好，日子总是过得忙碌而充实。

比山水更加绵长的，大概是邱凌和中国大好河山、新旧好友之间难以割舍
的情谊。

邱凌来到中国虽时间不长，却已经结交了很多本地好友，也积极参与海洋

学院主办的各种校园活动。他时常赞叹浙江大学"对留学生非常友好，有国际范儿"。在这融入的过程中，因为在同一间实验室、师从同一个导师，邱凌很快与中国博士生周多成了好朋友。对方已经结婚生子，经常邀请邱凌到他家做客，和妻儿共进晚餐。这对于独自在中国的留学生邱凌来说无疑是最大的善意与接纳。"我在刚来的第一周便学会了'你好''谢谢''多少钱'等基本中文单词，这多亏了周多和我众多热情友好的中国朋友们。汉语很难学，但也真的很有魅力。"此外邱凌向我介绍道，舟山校区校园中有很多国际化的活动，留学生和本地学生都可以参加。其中最令邱凌印象深刻的便是刚来到浙江大学时的那个冬天，他参加了人生中第一个元旦晚会。

"中国学生都是非常喜欢体验不同生活的，像去年的留学生元旦晚会就有很多中国学生参加。来自中国、美国、尼日利亚、坦桑尼亚的学生一起品尝美食，交流文化，其乐无穷。最有意思的是最后一个歌舞节目，每个人拿着不同

邱凌（第1排右3）在浙江大学海洋学院2018年元旦晚会上与外国留学生合影
Qiu Ling (front right 3rd) with the international students at the 2018 New Year's party, Ocean College, ZJU

颜色的国旗一起大合唱，那一瞬间，我真切感受到了文化的融合。"

嘹亮的歌声响彻舞会大厅，不同肤色、不同民族的学生一起载歌载舞，平日实验室里的同学和导师，那一刻都成了共享同一份快乐的朋友。这份独特的体验早已镌刻在了邱凌脑海里，成为他值得一生珍藏的回忆。

从巴基斯坦来到中国，相隔千里，跨越重洋。邱凌怀揣梦想远离了故乡的一切，将自己投掷进一种全新的生活可能性之中，却幸运地在这里寻找到了自己的第二故乡。在过去的五个月里，邱凌凭借着扎实的基本功和对科学的满腔热忱，为他在浙江大学海洋学院的研究事业开了个好头，而接下来的两年，他定会不负众望，脚踏实地继续前行。如果有机会的话，邱凌想研究生毕业后继续留在浙江大学读博士，为了祖国，为了理想，更为了这片在成长过程中给了他无限滋养的土地——中国，他的第二故乡。

在第二故乡扬帆起航，梦想在前方，而他，已经在路上。

采访人：王迎晓

采访日期：2018年3月

Starting Off from My Second Hometown

"As an international student studying at Zhejiang University, what kind of experience is it? "

"It is hard to cover in a few words, but on my first trip to China, I have already fallen in love with Zhoushan, and with ZJU!"

Brown skin, competent-looking short hair, and bright and intense eyes are the author's first impression on Qiu Ling. The simple reply speaks of his affection for China. Then, the story of Qiu Ling at ZJU is told in his melodious but fluent English, unfolding to me like a beautiful painting scroll. Qiu Ling is Aqeel Abbas' Chinese name.

From Pakistan to my second hometown——China

Qiu Ling, from Pakistan, is the only child in the family who studies abroad, and therefore has had its full support. Studying in China has been his long-cherished dream, and finally came true after he graduated from college. He traveled all the way across the ocean to a strange country, only to pursue his simple love and ideals.

"When I first arrived in China, my Chinese was not good enough. I worried about how to communicate with the locals, how to buy daily necessities, how to get around, and so on." But Qiu Ling's relaxed tone suggests his worries were largely unfounded. "Over time, my friends and I have learned to use mobile APPs such as Taobao, Alipay, WeChat and Didi, which make everything so easy and helps a great deal the international students in their daily life in China. Most supermarkets here accept mobile payments, but these high-tech products are not available in my home in Pakistan. The most amazing thing is that I can actually buy my own ethnic food on Taobao!" Through the lively description by Qiu Ling, we are pleased to see that he has long adapted to the life in China, and now behaves just like a "local boy". When asked about how to use Taobao when his Chinese is yet proficient, Qiu Ling grins proudly and shares me with his secrets: "I generally key in what I need in English to search for product pictures. I then compare the prices to decide which one to buy. It is actually very convenient."

As for the biggest differences between the life in Pakistan and in China, Qiu Ling said frankly: "For academic research, ZUJ has cutting-edge equipment in the specific fields, a

good research atmosphere and a higher platform; In everyday life, as I have just said, China's Internet is so developed that many times I can't help feeling sorry for my friends at home. Overall, China makes me feel strongly that everything is possible in this country."

Apart from being attracted to all aspects of academic and life, Qiu Ling also has a special liking for the natural beauty of China. He wants to appreciate it personally. "I have been to Beijing and Hangzhou for academic meetings. But because of the time limit, I did not see the Great Wall or the West Lake. I really hope that I can go there again. And I've already visited places of interests in Zhoushan with friends on weekends. The Moon Bay and Putuo Mountain are beautiful. But what I like Zhoushan most, is probably the ocean. In my hometown, it is almost impossible to see an ocean." At his words, I can almost picture the way the young Pakistani looks at the open sea—with his gaze focused on the unfathomable water, and also the lofty ideals shining together with the shimmering water.

For Qiu Ling, although China and Pakistan are so different, he loves both dearly. "I have always regarded China as my second hometown. She is not just a place, but more like a love complex. That was what I actually felt when I came to study at ZJU." From Qiu Ling's emotional revelation of his deep ties with China, I can perceive the longing and firmness in his eyes.

Starting off for his dream that began in ZJU.

Since Qiu Ling's interests are very much in line with the research direction of his current instructor, plus, there are more seminars and opportunities of the international exchange students at ZJU to improve in his research capabilities remarkably, Qiu Ling decided to choose ZJU as the starting point of his dream.

"To study in a top university like ZJU has been my dream all the time. The moment I received the admission letter, I was overjoyed." Recalling the scene at that time, Qiu Ling seems very excited, as if it has been brought back to the day when his story began, "Imagine on my first trip to China, I met some international friends from all over the world. I have the opportunity to study with them in one of the best universities in China. How lucky I am!"

And the most unforgettable thing for Qiu Ling is his first day at ZJU. According to him, meeting everyone was like joining a warm family. "It was my first time to meet my instructor, Dr. Li Chunfeng and the fellow students of the 'marine geophysics and geodynamics' research group. Because of some academic requirements, I arrived a month later than I had scheduled, and missed the whole course of the winter semester. So my instructor said to me, 'if you don't have classes this semester, then why don't you go to Beijing to attend a seminar?' So, together with another international student, Akinrinade Opeyemi, I went to an academic conference of Professor Amous Nur of Stanford University held in Beijing's Tsinghua University." Talking about this experience, Qiu Ling is full of gratitude to his instructor. "It was a very memorable experience and a good learning platform. It gave me some new ideas for my future research, thanks to my instructor, Mr. Li Chunfeng."

When talking about his beloved student Qiu Ling, Dr. Li immediately put on a proud smile. "Qiu Ling, as an international student, sometimes even works harder than some Chinese students. The overall impression he leaves to us is that he is not impetuous but steady and quiet, and above all, extremely dedicated to study." Li also holds great expectations for Qiu Ling's academic achievements in the graduate program, which, he believes, will benefit enormously both Pakistan's maritime cause and the relations between the country and China.

In addition to Dr. Li's unreserved help, the care from his classmates has also been the cornerstone of Qiu Ling's progress. "Here I have met many Chinese friends working in the same discipline. When I have a problem, I can always find a solution. And what particularly makes me at home is that I see my compatriots here in China: Khan, Madaba, Ishiha and Farhan. The help from my Pakistani folks is most heartwarming."

Back in Pakistan, Qiu Ling's mother tongue is Urdu. Therefore for him, the constant practice in both English and Chinese is vital. He is currently majoring in marine geology and geophysics, with specific research in the application of submarine seismometers to study the deep structure of the South China Sea Basin. This is a subject even a Chinese student finds challenging. But in Qiu Ling's eyes, he "has had hardly any difficulties." When the author, out of curiosity, probes him for tips, he reveals his magic. "The professors and fellow Chinese classmates here are always ready to help me in my study. They often take an active interest in me. I have the opportunities to learn from everyone. In such an environment of mutual help and assistance, I hardly feel bothered by resistance and difficulties and have never complained about the hardships in study."

If Qiu Ling's career in academics is a sailing boat of dream poised for a long voyage, then ZJU is where his dreams begin. While Qiu Ling's hometown is the harbor where he seeks refuge when feeling tired and confused, the teachers and classmates he has met along the way are like the much needed wind. Their ceaseless help has been a powerful morale booster. The sailboat is about to set off. Even though it has to battle through wind and waves, it will not

hesitate to push ahead.

Deep and lasting friendship

My Chinese name "Qiu Ling" is inspired by Chinese landscape. That heaven-like place has all the natural attractions that you can imagine, peaks, lakes, islands. My friends from my motherland and the friendly Chinese people who make me feel at home are like the mountains that I can lean and depend on.

Outside the busy academic life, visiting different parts of the world is a major hobby of Qiu Ling. When traveling, he can always meet interesting people and things, some trivial, some grand. The greatness and mendacity constantly intertwined to enrich his understanding of the globe. Having been in China for half a year, Qiu Ling hardly feels homesick, because he has friends among the overseas students in many cities in China. He travels to their cities in the holidays, sight-seeing and reinforcing the friendship. He is always busy and full-scheduled.

Qiu Ling loves China's rivers and mountains and treasures the friendship with his friends, whether old or new.

Although not in China for long, Qiu Ling has already made a lot of local friends. An active participant in the campus events hosted by the Ocean College, he often commends ZJU for its kindness to the international students as befitting a top international institute. In the process of integration, he quickly becomes fast friends with Zhou Duo, a Chinese PhD candidate working in the same laboratory and under the instructorship of the same professor. Zhou is married and has a child. He often invites Qiu Ling to his place for dinner with his family. This is undoubtedly seen as the greatest goodwill and acceptance for the young Pakistani who lives alone in China. "I learned the basic Chinese expressions like 'hello' 'thank you' 'how much' within my first week of arrival, thanks to Zhou Duo and many of my warm and kind Chinese friends. Chinese is very difficult, but it is also very charming."

Furthermore, Qiu Ling explains to me that there are many international events on the Zhoushan campus, open to both international and local students. What has impressed Qiu Ling most is the winter when he went to the first New Year's party in China.

"Chinese students are very fond of different life experiences. At the 2018 New Year's party for the international students, many Chinese students attended, eating and having fun with the students from the US, Nigeria and Tanzania. It was great. The most interesting part was the last song and dance show, when all the people came together for a big chorus, each holding a flag of a different nation. At that moment, I keenly felt the powerful fusion of cultures."

The loud singing reverberated through the dance hall. Students of different skin colors and nationalities sang and danced together. The students and instructors in the laboratory became friends on the equal footing, sharing the same happy moment. This unique experience has long been imprinted in the minds of Qiu Ling as a lifetime memory.

From Pakistan to China, that is a journey covering thousands of miles, across the oceans. Qiu Ling, leaving his hometown far behind to pursue a dream, has resolutely thrown himself to a new possibility of life, and luckily and unexpectedly found his second home in the East. In the past five months, he has made a good start for his research in the Ocean College of ZJU by relying on his solid previous learning and his passion for science. In the next two years, he will definitely live up to his expectations and strive for more success. If there is a chance, Qiu Ling would like to continue his stay at ZJU after graduation to pursue a doctorate degree. It is a grand target he sets for the sake of his motherland, his ideal, and more for China, the vast land that has nurtured him in his growth, the country he regards as his second hometown.

The dream-fulfilling long voyage from his second hometown has already begun.

浙里四年，硕果累累

与浙江大学相遇、相知、相熟的这一段时光，对于来自毛里求斯的碧碧来说，是人生中一段鲜亮而有趣的旅程。旅途中，她与老师和同学们相伴同行，在海洋药物学中探索奥秘。她如蚌壳中的珍珠，在打磨中不断收获属于自己的耀眼光芒。

四年的时间看似很长，但却转瞬即逝。虽然不久前刚刚毕业，但对于碧碧来说，旅程仍未止，与浙大的缘分仍未尽。

与海相伴的思与行

浙江大学海洋学院博士生导师吴斌教授曾去过毛里求斯进行科研采样工作，他对这个民风淳朴、教育先进的国家很有好感。他的学生碧碧就是来自这个大学教育与西方接轨的国家，并在当地最好的大学——毛里求斯大学接受了海洋科学与技术方面的良好教育。

勤奋努力的碧碧在专业成绩上名列前茅，并顺利被浙江大学海洋学院录取。在选择浙大之前，她其实已经获得了英国和南非的奖学金及深造机会，但是由于对中国的好感，她还是决定放弃那两个机会，漂洋过海来到中国。

她在中国的学习同样延续了以往的勤奋与刻苦。吴斌教授称赞道："碧碧不仅有着比较优秀的专业基础，更是在学习上下了不少工夫，和其他留学生相比，她花在学习上的时间差不多是别人的两倍以上！"在实验室中常常能够看到这样的景象，许多中国学生已经做完实验离开了，但是碧碧仍留在实验室中继续着。在实验期间，碧碧待在实验室的时间往往都在八个小时以上，每晚离开时都与十点的星光相伴，有时甚至会更晚。

碧碧在浙江大学海洋学院2018年元旦晚会上
Bibi at the 2018 New Year's Party, Ocean College, ZJU

她说："学习时间的长短是由你自己想要学习的内容多少来决定的。"带着学习的激情与对知识的渴求，碧碧取得了很大的收获。碧碧十分喜欢找自己的导师交流沟通，除了在专业知识上和老师一起钻研，更在学习过程中学会了看待事物的不同方式，锻炼了自己的批判性思维。这让她受益良多。

行与思，是碧碧在浙大学习生活中的两大法宝。在科研中必不可少的动手实验、不断尝试，是她总结经验、磨炼性格的过程；而与导师和同学们的交流中出现的思维碰撞、想法创新，也对她的学习工作带来潜移默化的深远影响。与海相伴，且行且思，碧碧在浙江大学这个包容开放的环境中一路成长。

汉语学习的苦与乐

碧，意指青绿色的玉石或青绿色。江淹《别赋》有记载：春草碧色，春水绿波。碧碧的中文名恰如其人。她有着绿草般的激情与活力，有着翠玉般的坚实与勇敢。她笑着说，这个中文名是她的中文老师为她取的，她非常喜欢。

碧碧来到中国后，收获的可不只是美丽的中文名字，还有一段特别的汉语学习经历。碧碧来到浙大的第一年是在玉泉校区学习中文，一年后才去舟山校区海洋学院学习。刚来到浙大时，碧碧对汉语一头雾水，在学习和生活上遇到了不少问题。于是她投入了大量时间进行学习，以提高自己的中文水平。上午8:00—11:00是碧碧的汉语学习时间，从拼音到语法，从口语到听力，碧碧都勤奋练习。经过一年的中文学习后，她欣喜地感受到自己在交流上突然轻松起来了。

　　这样的变化，不仅是碧碧自己不断努力的结果，她在这里遇见的中国老师和同学们也功不可没。碧碧直言："来到舟山后，我觉得自己的中文水平有了更加突飞猛进的提高，这里的外国留学生比起杭州少了许多，所以在课程学习中我需要更多地和中国的实验室伙伴交流，和中国的教授们交流，这些锻炼让我能够更加自信地去表达了！"除了校内的交流，碧碧有时还会用中文和超市里的人聊天，她说这也是她学中文的秘诀之一。

　　谈到自己现在的中文水平，碧碧笑着用中文"自夸"了一句："还可以！马马虎虎。"在她看来，中文水平是自己一项宝贵的财富。在舟山时，留学生同学需要外出时很喜欢叫上碧碧同行，因为她可以帮忙做一些交流和翻译。在吴斌教授看来，碧碧的中文水平十分不错，有时还打趣地让她给大家传授一下学中文的经验方法。他称赞道，"她的中文和一般留学生相比更好一些，我常开玩笑，有些中国同学学了十几年英语都没能精通，而碧碧能用一年时间就把中文学得这么好，真是十分难得的。"

碧碧（中间）在浙江大学海洋学院参加马拉松比赛时与队友合影
Bibi (middle) with other team members in the marathon
competition of Ocean College, ZJU

海洋生物的宝藏

作为海洋药物学专业的学生，碧碧主要的研究方向是海洋药物学。她在浙大的科研项目就是在海洋的微生物中寻找一些有价值、有效用的物质，并取得了十分重要的研究成果——在海洋的一种真菌中发现了两种非常特殊的抗生素。这两种抗生素对大部分的耐药菌都可以产生作用，在医学领域具有很大的应用前景，未来可以用作药品开发的原材料或者其他用途。吴斌教授说："虽然目前这两种抗生素离最后制作药物、变成成品仍有一段很长的距离，但它们在当前研究中展现出的杀菌特性已经奠定了它们未来的发展价值。"

这样宝贵的发现是来之不易的。从最原始的初期采样，到从样品中分离出微生物，再到分离出其中的化合物，乃至最后研究出这些化合物的化学结构以及药理活性，这一整套过程都是碧碧在导师的指导下独立完成的，它们凝聚了碧碧许多日夜的心血与付出。

实验最初的采样是在舟山朱家尖的海滩上。吴斌回忆道："当时我只负责将他们送到海边，剩下所有的工作都需要他们自己独立完成，我发现碧碧的动手能力是很不错的。"比起采样，繁复而漫长的分离过程更加具有挑战性。当

时这个实验组的微生物分离工作就历时了好几个月，这项工作就像在茫茫沙漠中寻找沙砾中的钻石，在几百块拼图中找寻正确的那一块一样，其所需的耐心与细心可想而知。"这个过程中会出现很多意想不到的困难与问题，有时候你花了很多时间分离出一种物质，但最终发

碧碧取得硕士研究生学位照片
Bibi receiving her Master's degree

现它是没有实际效果的。在这种情况下，就只能继续努力，不能放弃。"碧碧如是说。

碧碧的发现和因此产出的多篇论文成果与导师的帮助是密不可分的。在她进行实验以及学习的每一个步骤中，一旦遇到问题，都可以在导师那里获得及时有效的帮助。"甚至是在假期这样的时间里，他也能及时回复我的邮件。"除了导师，还有许多老师给碧碧留下了深刻印象，"我遇见过一些中文授课的老师，他们并不擅长说英文，但是每回我咨询问题时，他们总是会尽可能地回复并且努力说英文来方便我理解。"

最终，碧碧克服了众多的困难，成功发现了这两种宝贵的抗生素。在2017年度海洋学院优秀学生奖学金评比中，碧碧成了唯一获此殊荣的留学生。虽然目前她已经毕业，但吴斌教授计划让接下来的同学将这两个发现继续深入研究下去，并且在之后申请相关的专利。

人生旅途的转弯口

2018年3月，碧碧从浙江大学海洋学院正式毕业，取得了硕士研究生的学位。对于她来说，这是人生一个关键的转弯口。

她回想起自己在中国的这四年时光。在北京蜿蜒千里、雄奇壮观的长城上的某些古老斑驳的砖块上曾有过她的足迹；在上海五光十色、繁华缤纷的都市里某一块光洁亮丽的镜面中曾倒映过她的身影；在义乌热闹熙攘、人群拥挤的市场里某一个精致的手工艺品曾吸引过

碧碧获得浙江大学海洋学院优秀学生荣誉
Bibi being awarded the Excellent Student of Ocean College, ZJU

她的注意……而更多的时候，她在杭州西湖边的步道上漫步，在玉泉校区高大的梧桐树下走过，在舟山校区安静的图书馆中阅读。这趟在中国、在浙大的旅程丰富而精彩。

现在，碧碧对未来的计划是继续深造，完成博士研究生学业，在海洋药物这个自己喜爱的专业上取得更高的成就。临近毕业时，她已经获得英国华威的全额校长奖学金可以在那里攻读博士学位。但她目前尚未决定好最终深造的地点，仍在继续斟酌适合自己研究方向的高校以及奖学金项目，浙大也在她的选择之列。

她满含眷恋地感慨道："杭州是一个如此美丽便捷的城市，浙大的学术环境也十分优越，老师们更是能给予我很好的引领与指导，在这里的四年让浙大成了我第二个家一样的存在，如果有机会能在这里继续我的学业，我为什么要说不呢？"碧碧边说边笑了起来。

从浙大海洋学院硕士毕业是碧碧人生中的转折点，不论接下来的旅途是继续与浙江大学相伴前行，还是去到世界的其他角落，她和中国、和浙江大学的缘分都不会就此终结，而是会更加长远。

采访人：陆理宁

采访日期：2018年3月

The Fruitful Four Years in Zhejiang University

For Bibi from Mauritius, the time after she came to Zhejiang University and after she got acquainted to and became familiar with it was delightful and interesting, in which she has traveled with her teachers and classmates to explore the mysteries of marine pharmacology. Like a pearl in an oyster shell, she keeps polishing herself to harvest her own dazzling shininess.

Four years may seem too long, but it's fleeting. Although she has already finished her study not long ago, for Bibi, the journey is still not over and her predestined tie with ZJU has not come to an end.

Love the ocean and live for it

Professor Wu Bin, a doctoral instructor of the Ocean College of ZJU, was once in Mauritius for research sampling, and has had a favorable impression on this island nation, where the people are simple and unsophisticated, yet the education is advanced and westernized. His student Bibi is precisely from the country, well educated in the University of Mauritius, the best local institution of higher learning, especially competent in marine science and technology.

Bibi, a diligent girl and top achiever in her discipline, has been admitted by the Ocean College of ZJU. Before choosing the university, she had already won the scholarship and further study opportunities in Britain and South Africa. But because of her love for China, she decided to forgo them and travelled across the ocean to China.

In China, she has continued her previous diligence and assiduity. "Bibi does not only have a solid professional foundation, but also works very hard. Compared with some other foreign students, Bibi spends almost twice as much time studying!" so marveled Professor Wu. It's a common scene of her busy days in the lab. Many Chinese students would leave the lab after the experiment session is over, but Bibi stays on. On average, she works more than eight hours in the lab during the experiments, often leaving at 10 p.m., sometimes even later."

"The amount of time you spend on study is determined by how much you want to learn," she says. With a passion for learning and a thirst for knowledge, Bibi has gained even more than she expected. She enjoys communicating with her instructor. Besides studying with her professors academically, she has come to look at things in different perspectives. Such training in critical thinking benefits her immensely.

Acting and thinking are her secrets to study well. The indispensable hands-on and constant trials in research are her ways of summarizing her experience and forging her personality. While the collision of ideas and innovative thinking in communicating with her instructor and fellow students also exert a profound and subtle influence on her. Accompanied by the ocean, through active thinking and action, Bibi grows steadily amid the inclusive and open environment of ZJU.

Joys and sorrows in the Chinese learning

In Chinese, the character "Bi" refers to green jade. Jiang Yan, a great poet in the 5th century AD, was a passionate lover of this color of grass and water in the season of spring. Bibi's Chinese name truthfully reflects her personality—full of the vigor and vitality of the sprouting green grass in the spring, of the hardness and unyielding nature of green jade. She claims proudly that the name is given by her Chinese teacher and she likes it very much.

Since in China, what Bibi has acquired far exceeds a pretty Chinese name. She has had in fact some unique experience in learning the language. Bibi spent her first year in ZJU learning Chinese on Yuquan campus, and went to the Ocean College in Zhoushan afterwards. During her early days in ZJU, Bibi was utterly confused with Chinese and had many problems in study and in life. So she invested a lot of time to improve her Chinese. From 8 am to 11 am, Bibi studied Chinese, from pinyin to grammar, from listening to speaking. Following a year of intensive linguistic training, she was pleased to discover that communications had suddenly become easier.

Such changes came not only from Bibi's own constant efforts, but also from the help of Chinese teachers and schoolmates. Bibi said frankly "after arriving in Zhoushan, I feel my Chinese has progressed by leaps and bounds. There are much fewer foreign students here than in Hangzhou. So in study I need to communicate more in Chinese with my lab partners and professors. But such forced training increases my confidence to express myself in Chinese." Besides communicating on campus, Bibi sometimes uses Chinese to chat with people in the supermarket, which she claims to be one of her secrets in upgrading Chinese.

Speaking of her current Chinese level, Bibi smiled and complimented herself in Chinese, "Hai Ke Yi, Ma Ma Hu Hu." (It's OK! Just so so.) In her opinion, her Chinese is a valuable asset. In Zhoushan, when a few international students need to go out, they would like to take

Bibi along, because she can help them with communication and translation. In Professor Wu's view, Bibi's Chinese is very good and he sometimes also jokingly asks her to share her method of learning. Professor Wu believes "Her Chinese is better than average international students. I often feel puzzled that some Chinese students spend over 10 years on learning English but cannot apply it skillfully. And it only takes Bibi a year to learn Chinese so well. It's just amazing."

Treasure trove of Marine life

As a student majoring in marine pharmacology, Bibi has her main research direction focused on the subject. Her research project in ZJU is to find valuable and effective substances in ocean microorganisms. She has made impressive achievements—two very special antibiotics have been found in a sea fungus. They can act on most drug-resistant bacteria, and thus promise great potential in pharmacology as they can be used as raw materials for drug development or other applications in the future. "Although the two antibiotics are still a long way from becoming the final product, the bactericidal properties they exhibit in the current study have shown their value for future development," Wu enthuses.

Such encouraging discoveries are hard-won. The whole process, from the initial sampling, to the sample separation of microorganisms, to the extraction of compounds, and finally to the studies of their chemical structure and pharmacological activity, has been completed independently by Bibi under the guidance of her instructor. Her prolonged and painstaking efforts have turned out fruition.

The initial sampling was performed on the beach of Zhujiajian, Zhoushan, Professor Wu recalls, "At that time, I was only responsible for dispatching them to the beach. All the rest of the work was to be done by themselves. I was impressed by Bibi's strong hands-on ability." Comparing to sampling, the complex and lengthy separation process was more challenging. It took months to isolate the microbes by this experimental group, a process demanding as much patience and attention as looking for a diamond in a vast sand desert or finding the right pieces in a huge jigsaw puzzle. "There were many unexpected difficulties and problems. Sometimes you spent a lot of time separating out a substance, only to find it of no practical value. In this case, you would have to keep on trying and not give up." Bibi said.

Bibi's findings and the number of research papers later produced were inseparable from her instructor's help. In each step of her experiments and learning, she could get immediate and effective help from Professor Wu whenever she encountered problems. "Even during times like holidays, he would respond to my emails in a most timely manner." Besides the instructor, many other teachers have also impressed Bibi deeply. "I have met some Chinese language teachers who are not good at spoken English. But every time I ask a question, they would always reply as best as they can in English to facilitate my understanding."

Finally, Bibi overcame numerous difficulties and succeeded in discovering these two valuable antibiotics. She was the only international student to receive the Ocean College's Outstanding Student Scholarship in 2017. After her graduation, Professor Wu plans to ask her classmates to further study the two findings and apply for relevant patents later.

Turning Point in Life

In March, Bibi formally graduated from ZJU's Ocean College with her Master's degree. For her, it is a key turning point in her life.

She looks back at her four years in China. In Beijing, she has been to the magnificent Great Wall stretching thousands of winding miles; In the dazzling streets of Shanghai, she has seen her image in the pieces of bright and clean mirrors. In Yiwu's bustling market, her attention was drawn to an exquisite handicrafts... More often, she promenades around Hangzhou's West Lake, strolls under the tall sycamores on ZJU's Yuquan campus, or loses herself in reading in the quiet library in Zhoushan. Her time in China and ZJU has been both colorful and fruitful.

Now Bibi's plan for the future is to pursue further studies, to complete a doctoral course, and to achieve higher results in her favorite discipline of marine medicine. At her graduation, she had been granted a full chancellor's scholarship for a PhD at Warwick of UK. But at present, she has not decided on the place for her final study, as she is still examining the universities and scholarship programs suitable for her research direction. ZJU is also among her choices.

Full of sentiments, she sighs with deep emotion, "Hangzhou is such a beautiful and convenient city. ZJU has top-class academic environment. What's more, the professors here are the most qualified to offer me excellent guidance and directions. ZJU has been my second home in the past four years. So if I am offered the opportunity to continue my study here, why would I want to say no?" Bibi laughs.

The graduation from ZJU Ocean College marks a turning point in Bibi's life. Whether her following journey continues here in ZJU or takes her to another corner of the world, her relationship with China and with ZJU will not end, and it will well last into the distant future.

留学于浙，筑梦成舟

2013年，缅甸丹老大学讲堂，当一位归国教授在台上分享着自己在中国、在浙大时的所见所感时，对于吉奥来说，理想大学中偌大优美的校园、设备先进的实验室、充满思维碰撞的图书馆和干净整洁的校舍，便不再只是脑海里遥不可及的梦。如果说教授的言辞为吉奥勾勒出了浙大的轮廓，那么师生亲友的鼓励、中国政府提供的MOFCOM奖学金，则是他决心来到"浙里"的最大动力。

2016年9月，杭州萧山国际机场，当来自缅甸的飞机着陆时，吉奥便知道承载着自己梦想和机遇的留学生涯即将开始了。

初来浙里：向往与现实

以前，吉奥只从网上或从他人口中了解过中国：那是一个面积广大、人口众多、经济发达的国家。直到第一次亲临杭州，他才真正地感受到这片土地和人们的温度。一下飞机，吉奥便得到了来自浙江大学国际学院的中国同学们的问候和接待，因而独自一人与陌生感带来的不知所措和担忧便消解了许多。开学前的入学注册等手续，也在志愿者们的帮助下顺利完成。谈到对杭州的第一印象，吉奥提到最多的无疑是"整洁、优雅"四个字：干净宽敞的街道和优美的风景，还有华家池校区里舒畅的环境与错落的建筑。这个城市的精致与发达的所有细节都给吉奥留下了深刻的印象。

"这里和我的国家，和我以前的学校太不一样了。"吉奥用淳朴的语言述

吉奥在舟山校区
Kyaw at Zhoushan
campus

说着他眼中的中国城市和校园。来到舟山校区，既承载着浙大历史，又孕育着新兴学科基地的海洋学院向他展现出它博物开怀、欣欣向荣的独特风貌。想到自己已然身处在世界顶尖大学之一的校园中，吉奥欢欣之时也暗下决心：应当努力成为不负所托的"灿若星辰的浙大人"。

在"浙里"，吉奥要攻读的是博士学位，因此选择具体的研究方向和对应的导师就显得尤为重要。吉奥现在的导师是吴嘉平教授，不过回想起最初研究方向的确定还颇历了一些周折。在被录取到海洋资源与环境专业后，吉奥的个人资料本被分配到了海洋资源研究所。这个所的主要研究方向是石油和矿产，然而这与他之前研究的海洋生物学相距甚远。好在通过学院的帮助和引导，以及和教授们的几次探讨交流，吉奥终于联系到了与他研究背景相符的吴嘉平教授。在经历转导师的流程后，吉奥顺利成为吴教授实验室里国籍独特的"门生"之一。

成长于浙：师友相伴，苦乐随行

对于吉奥来说，浙大舟山校区的多媒体教学设备先进、实验室设施齐全、宿舍条件完善，学习和生活都有着充分的硬件保障。但是，如同从缅甸到中国辗转而来的路途，吉奥的留学生涯也不总是一帆风顺的，尤其是在语言沟通和文化差异上。由于吉奥的母语是缅甸语，而浙大的课程几乎都是用中文或英文授课的，所以需要同时熟练地掌握并运用英文和中文对他来说是个很大的挑战。不过，好在有老师及同学的热心帮助，从刚入校时的选课操作指导到课后的交流学习，从汉字的拼音字母到正确的中文发音，如今他已经熟悉了中文，掌握了不少词句。

提起老师，吉奥说最要感激的是自己的导师吴嘉平教授，他不仅在科研上十分细致耐心地给予自己指导，在生活方面也对自己关照有加。由于吴教授本人也曾到国外留学，对其中遇到的各种困难和迷茫感同身受，因此他对实验室里的留学生们倍加关怀，比如让中国同学一对一地指导他们选课、进行语言学习和课业上的帮助，在节假日时鼓励他们参加校区活动或小聚，以免身在异国他乡时会太想家。

在吴教授的眼里，吉奥是一个好学上进而又勤奋朴实的学生。在语言学习方面，除了师友的帮助，吉奥自己也会在课后下许多工夫：不仅认真研读老师给的参考资料，还会主动去做练习，以努力缩小和其他同学的差距。在学术研究上，面对自己相对薄弱的学科基础知识和新研究带来的未知挑战，他会选择泡在图书馆里阅读更多的书；在实验和数据分析上，他更主动地向导师请教，与中国同学一同探讨；在外出采样时，他会做更充分细致的准备。面对学术钻研本身所强调的科学性和创新性，他展现出了自己一如既往的热情和专注。

吉奥和同学们一起学习中国书法
Kyaw learning Chinese calligraphy with his classmates

在新年晚会上演唱的吉奥
Kyaw singing at the New
Year's party

　　吉奥坦言，自己曾经是一个容易"害羞"的人，在许多人面前说话或演讲时会紧张和不安。因此，刚来浙大上课时，他对老师要求每位同学都需要上台做展示的任务感到有些不知所措。好在经过一年多的时光，在浙大多元化考核模式的要求下，他在不断的尝试和挑战中打磨自己——大到确定一篇讲稿的逻辑框架，小到一字一句的腔调发音，对自我的更高要求和不断超越成就了如今更加自信的他。

　　这份自信不但让吉奥如今能胸有成竹地站在众人面前展示自己，发表演讲，也让他在"浙里"的生活更加丰富多彩。吉奥热爱音乐，来到中国后尤其喜欢一些中文歌曲优美而恬淡的旋律，因此听音乐和做运动成了他缓解压力、释放情绪的最佳方式。而这份对音乐的热爱让他在学院的新年晚会上一展歌喉，用一首 *All of Me* 打动了观众，也促使他成为实验室里出了名的"行走的歌王"。爱唱歌的特质让他交到了更多来自世界各国的朋友，在彼此的交往中，吉奥也更深切地感受到了在这个开放包容的校园里，不同种族、不同国籍的同学们身上所体现的多元文化和其散发出的光芒与魅力。

筑梦于浙：无憾亦无悔

　　现在，吉奥研究的课题方向是"红树林固碳"，这对于他来说既是兴趣使然，更是挑战所在。由于缅甸大部分地区为热带季风气候，得天独厚的地理环境孕育了大片的原生红树林，它们是应对全球气候变化的重要资源。然而，缅甸国内相关方面的研究甚少，对其价值及应用更是缺乏深度挖掘。因此，吉奥希望能以这个课题为契机，毕业后依据自己国家的实际情况为世界环境生态问题做一些富有实效的贡献。如今，项目的设计和采样阶段已经完成。接下来，他要进行样品处理和分析，得出具体的实验数据，撰写分析报告，潜心学问。做科研最讲究的便是要"沉得住气"，虽然吉奥不似其他人那样早早在期刊上发表论文，但相信在不久的将来，吉奥将会带着令人满意的成果回到自己的国家。

在浙大近两年的时光里，在尝过了留学生活的苦与乐之后，吉奥感慨自己对科研、大学和国家的体悟多了许多。除却校园内外的一幅幅生活场景，在"浙里"培养的学术精神、师生情谊和家国情怀将成为他人生中最重要的一座桥梁。"浙大是一个能让青年人实现梦想的地方。"说这句话的时候，吉奥托着腮，目光深邃而真挚。

谈到未来的目标和梦想，吉奥说自己将继续科研的道路，深入"固碳"的

为实验采集土壤样本的吉奥
Kyaw collectiing soil samples for experiment

吉奥（左2）与课题组成员在一起
Kyaw (left 2nd) with other team members

原理和渠道，并回到国内成为一名讲师、教授。同时，有感于中国政府对教育资金的投入和对大学的建设，他会努力尝试让缅甸教育部对高校予以更多的重视，建立完善的设施和实验体系，为学术研究和人才培养创造良好条件。除此之外，他还会像当初那位站在母校讲堂上的教授那样，把自己在浙大的求学经历和感悟分享于众，鼓励更多的学生来中国、到"浙里"，看看浙大的校园、舟山的大桥、杭州的西湖和中国的壮美山河、独特的风土人情，并告诉他们："浙大能为你铺一条科研之路，打开一扇梦想之门。"

说起梦想，有时候它其实并不需要特别高远，而是需要一如既往的坚持和脚踏实地的奋斗。一如吉奥在采访当天穿着的浅蓝色衬衫，朴实的努力是他丈量未来的脚步，亦是他驶向梦想的航船。从"浙里"出发，无极无终。

采访人：李佳荫

采访日期：2018年3月

Study in Zhejiang University to Build a Dream

One day in 2013, in a lecture hall of Myanmar's Mergui University, a professor went on the podium to share with his students his recent visit to China and particularly to Zhejiang University. Among the audience, Kyaw found his ideal university was no longer a distant dream, the spacious and magnificent campus, the laboratory with advanced facilities, the library full of thinking collisions, and the teaching buildings in a clean and tidy setting, etc. If the professor's story gave Kyaw a general idea of ZJU, the encouragement of his teachers, fellow students and his family, above all, the generous MOFCOM scholarship offered by the Chinese government, were the powerful motivations for his decision to come to ZJU.

When the plane from Myanmar landed in Hangzhou's Xiaoshan International Airport in September 2016, Kyaw knew that his life as a foreign student, with its dreams and opportunities, was about to begin.

Early days at ZJU: expectations and reality

In the past, Kyaw only learned about China on the Internet or from others: a large, populous and economically developing country. He didn't really felt the temperature of the land and people until his first visit to Hangzhou. Once off the plane, Kyaw was greeted and received by the Chinese students from the International College, which dissolved much of the confusion and worries resulted from being alone in a strange place. Helped by volunteers, pre-school registration and other formalities were completed without a hitch. When it comes to his first impression on Hangzhou, "neat and elegant" is undoubtedly the most frequent expression used by Kyaw: so many clean and spacious streets and beautiful natural sights, as well as the pleasing environment and tastefully planned buildings on Huajiachi campus. The exquisite and prosperous details of the city have impressed him deeply.

"It's so different from my country and from my former school." Kyaw speaks honestly of how he sees Chinese cities and campuses. On Zhoushan campus, the Ocean College, which not only bears the history of ZJU, but also nurtures the foundation of the emerging disciplines, greeted him with its uniquely rich, inclusive and thriving features. Realizing with delight that he was already a member of one of the world's top universities, Kyaw made up his mind: live up to high expectations by ranking himself among the "brilliant ZJU talents".

At ZJU, Kyaw studies for his PhD degree so that a specific research direction and corresponding instructor is particularly important. Kyaw's current instructor is Professor Wu Jiaping. The selection of his research direction initially ran into some difficulties: After he was admitted to the discipline of marine resources and environment, Kyaw's file was transferred to the Institute of Marine Resources whose main research focuses on oil and minerals, far different from his previous field of marine biology. Fortunately, with the help and guidance of the College leadership and after consultations with the faculty, Professor Wu, who shares a similar research background, was finally made available. Following the transfer process, Kyaw successfully became one of the students of different nationalities in the professor's laboratory team.

Grow up with pains and joys at ZJU

For Kyaw, Zhoushan campus of ZJU boasts advanced multimedia teaching equipment, complete laboratory facilities and good lodging conditions, offering sufficient hardware guarantee for the school life. However, just like the long journey from Myanmar to China, the overseas study life of Kyaw is not always smooth, especially in language communication and cultural differences. Since Kyaw's native language is Burmese, and almost all of ZJU's courses are taught either in Chinese or English, the ability to master and use the two languages skillfully proves to be a big challenge for him. Fortunately, the warm-hearted assistance of his teachers and fellow students—from the course selection to the communication after classes, from the Chinese characters' phonetic alphabets to their correct pronunciation—help him win the day. He is now familiar with Chinese language and knows a lot of useful expressions.

Speaking of the professors, Kyaw felt most indebted to his instructor Professor Wu, who does not only give him meticulous and patient guidance in research, but also takes care of him in life. The professor's own experience in studying abroad offers him better insight into the confusions and difficulties one is likely to encounter in a strange country. And he shows more care to his international students, such as encouraging Chinese students to provide additional one-on-one guidance in course selection, language learning and academic research. International students are also invited to campus activities or friend parties during the holidays so they would not feel too homesick in an alien land.

In Professor Wu's eyes, Kyaw is a studious and diligent student. To learn the languages well, aside from the assistance of the teachers and friends, Kyaw himself would put in grueling hours after class. He does not only study carefully the reference materials recommended by the teachers, but also takes the initiatives to drill more to narrow the gap with other students. In academic research, he would camp himself in the library reading to meet the unknown challenges brought both by his relatively weak academic foundation and a possible new subject. For experiment and data analysis, he actively seeks to consult with his instructor and Chinese fellow students. Before going on a sampling trip, he makes thorough preparations. As always, Kyaw shows his passion for and dedication to the scientific and innovative nature of academic research.

Kyaw admits that he used to be a "shy person" and often felt nervous when speaking in public. When he first came to ZJU, he would feel at loss over the presentation that every student has to do on the podium. Fortunately, after a year, pressed by the diversified assessment requirement in ZJU, he has finally trained himself well for the task in the wake of endless trials and challenges—from the structuring of logic framework of a speech to the right pronunciation of individual words. Higher self-demand and non-stop transcendence has boosted his self-confidence.

This confidence not only enables Kyaw to present himself in front of the public and give speeches, but also makes his life in ZJU more colorful. Kyaw loves music. After arriving in China, he has taken to the beautiful and tranquil melodies of a number of Chinese songs. Hence, listening to music and doing sports become the best ways for him to relieve the pressure and release his emotions. His love for music inspired him to sing at the College New Year's party, touching the audience with the song *All of Me* and earning him the title of "walking singer" in the lab. The passion for singing has also brought him more friends from all over the world. By communicating with them, Kyaw keenly feels, on this open and inclusive campus, the cultural diversity with its brilliance appealing to the students from different races and nationalities.

Dream-chasing at ZJU

Now, Kyaw's research subject is mangrove carbon sequestration, a field both interesting and challenging to him. Since Myamnar mostly enjoys a tropical monsoon climate, such uniquely advantageous geographical environment has given birth to a large area of native mangroves, which are an important resource for coping with global climate change. However, there is little research on relevant topics in Myanmar, especially in the in-depth exploration of the value and application. Therefore, Kyaw hopes, after his graduation, to take this project as an opportunity to make some effective contributions to the world's environmental and ecological problems based on the situation of his country. The design and sampling phase of the project is now completed. Next, he will conduct sample processing and analysis, obtain specific experimental data, write analysis report, and devote himself to relevant studies. The most important thing in scientific research is to have patience and persistence. Although Kyaw has not published papers in academic journals as early as some other people, he will no doubt return to his country with satisfactory results in the near future.

After the pains and gains of being a foreign student in the past two years at ZJU, Kyaw believes he has gained more insights into the concept of scientific research and of the university and the country. Apart from the lively scenes of life on and off the campus, the ZJU-cultivated academic spirit, the friendship between teachers and students, and the feelings of family and country will become the most important bridge in his life. "ZJU is a place where young people realize their dreams." When he utters this, Kyaw has a deep, sincere look on his face.

Relating to his future goals and dreams, Kyaw promises to continue his research, delve into the principles and channels of "carbon sequestration", and return to his country to become a lecturer and professor. At the same time, thanks to the education fund from the Chinese government and the current trend in strengthening the university education, he will try to convince the Ministry of Education of Myanmar to pay more attention to the institutions of higher learning, establish better facilities and experimental system, and create favorable conditions for research and talent cultivation. In addition, he will also be acting like the professor earlier in the lecture hall of his alma mater to share his experience at ZJU with everyone and encourage more students to come to China, to ZJU, to see its campus, the sea-spanning bridge of Zhoushan, the West Lake of Hangzhou, and other Chinese scenic sites, and to learn about the country's unique conditions and customs. He would tell them: "ZJU clears your way of doing research and open up a door to your dream."

With dreams, sometimes they don't need to be particularly lofty, but persistent and down-to-earth. Just like the plain light blue shirt that Kyaw wears on the day of the interview, the simple and solid efforts are his steps to measure the future, and are like the ship to carry his dream, sailing from ZJU to infinity.

后 记
Postscript

　　"所有困难都是生活的馈赠，所有经历都是人生的财富。"我想，在你读完这本书中的故事后，或许会对这句话有新的感悟。

　　在书中20位主人公讲述的故事中，有初来中国时对生活方式与文化习惯不同的困惑，有克服困难、逐渐适应并融入环境的喜悦，有因学习中文和了解中国后对中华文化的喜爱，有感受到中国经济的迅猛发展和中国人民的热情友善后希望成为中国连接世界的友好使者的愿望……也正是这些留学生思想上的蜕变和形形色色的留学轶事，交织成了书中的五味杂陈和多样人生。

　　其实，对于孕育这些故事的浙江大学海洋学院来说，这些蜕变是自然而然，并且仍在继续发生着的。自2012年中国政府海洋奖学金设立以来，作为首批试点四所高校之一，浙江大学海洋学院就围绕"海洋强国"和"21世纪海上丝绸之路"的战略布局，携手自然资源部第二海洋研究所，努力提升学院的国际化办学水平，促进我国与"海上丝路"沿线国家开展海洋领域的科教合作，共筑"合作之海""和谐之海"。同时，作为一所以"高起点、强辐射、可持续、国际化"为发展理念的专业型、研究型学院，浙江大学海洋学院主动在生源选拔、培养环节等方面积极探索，创新性地提出了"涉海留学生'OCEANS'六位一体人才培养体系"，并深入践行。原国家海洋局评价浙江大学为"培育方式最佳，最具有创新思维的学校"，认为浙江大学海洋学院"在配合我局工作、落实国家相关战略、提高人才培养力度、加强项目组织管理等方面均作出了突出贡献"。此项留学生培养项目在短时间内取得了较好成效，并在2016年获得了浙江省教学成果奖二等奖、浙江大学教学成果奖一等奖。可见，浙江大学海洋学院留学生教育教学改革的决心和用心。

海洋孕育了生命、连通了世界、促进了发展。对于远道而来的莘莘学子，除了让他们感知全人类一脉相承的"海洋命运共同体"，也需要他们更好地融入中国这片热土。传播他们的中国故事，让他们发挥"民间外交官"作用，是我们编辑这本书的初衷。

历史的轨迹总是从无到有，从少到多。浙江大学海洋学院也是经历了从2013年第一次招生时只有2名留学生，到如今在校留学的研究生有59人、毕业22人，成为浙江大学工科类、信息类院系中招收留学生最多的学院。不仅在生源数量上，学院对留学生的培养体系也有了质的转变，培养类型涵盖了博士和硕士研究生，生源国家从2个增加到21个，留学生的学术水平、科研能力和解决实际科学和工程问题的能力显著提升，高水平、高质量、高层次的科研成果逐渐涌现，赢得了留学生及其所在国的称赞。

"十年树木百年树人"，来华留学生是未来的中华文化使者，是中国文化洒向世界的种子，希望他们在中国土地上写下更多生动精彩的故事，让留学生的"洋青春"在中国文化里绽放，在中国开拓属于他们自己的"中国梦"。

为了讲好中国故事，传播好中国声音，我们征集了这20个故事，并附上故事的英文版，希望能获得读者的共鸣。本书从方案的构思到落地执行，最终得以顺利完成，要感谢原国家海洋局的大力支持，感谢浙江大学研究生院的持续关注，感谢浙江大学党委原常务副书记、海洋学院筹建工作领导小组组长陈子辰教授的全程引领，感谢浙江大学党委副书记朱世强教授和副校长王立忠教授的悉心指导，感谢浙江大学国际教育学院卢正中副院长、海洋学院王晓萍教授和马忠俊教授的鼎力相助，感谢浙江大学本科生采访团队对20个故事的用心整理，感谢受访留学生导师的积极协助并对故事内容认真核对，感谢海洋学院张誉译老师、谢程程老师、虞佳茜老师、胡小倩老师的热情帮助，感谢浙江大学外语学院李淑敏老师等为故事做的翻译工作，感谢为本书辛勤付出的工作人员。同时也感谢正在阅读本书的您！祝大家生活幸福温润、诗意盈怀。

陈丽

2019年6月28日